PRAISE FOR
Looking for Lydia; Looking for God

"A delicious read. Dean Robertson's *Looking for Lydia; Looking for God* tells the story of a journey—individual, historical and spiritual—through the post-Civil War South and the Bible studies that weave together the lives of a group of women at the Lydia H. Roper Home of Norfolk, Virginia. The result is an unusual and affecting tale of aging, community and personal obsession."

—Adam Sachs, Editor in Chief of *Saveur magazine.*

"As I read *Looking for Lydia* I weep. I want to read this book again and again. It's a conversation happening on the page, with Lydia, with all readers and searchers who share life through the stories we share."

—wendymarty@readingefficiencyprograms.com, Academic Coach, Reading Consultant, Learning Assistance Professional at Aquinas College, Grand Rapids, MI, and Grand Rapids Public Schools

"Storytelling at its finest. Dean Robertson uses the ancient stories of the Bible to inspire intellectual curiosity and reflection on their own life stories among a group of elderly southern women. Added to this is the tantalizing mystery of the historically elusive Lydia Roper for whom the women's retirement home is named."

—Susan Reigler, author, *Kentucky Bourbon Country* and *The Complete Guide to Kentucky State Parks*

"As a writer, an elder care giver, and a seeker of family stories, sharing this quest with Dean has been a glorious multi-faceted adventure. Readers will find that, whether they seek a lost relative or answers to Life's biggest questions, *Looking for Lydia* may lead them to find that exploring the questions can be as satisfying as finding the answers."

—Molly Roper Jenkins, Great-granddaughter of Lydia Bowen Roper

"Part biography, part biblical criticism, and part spiritual confession, *Looking for Lydia; Looking for God* is both an intensely personal narrative and an invitation to re-examine our collective soul. Humorous yet insightful, in this book, Robertson raises important questions of faith and meaning with her characteristic warmth and integrity. Perhaps, most importantly of all, it is a good read."

—Aaron Brittain, Rector, Talbot Park Baptist Church, Norfolk, VA

"A group of old ladies living together on the poorer side of health and finances, a few of whom aren't sure why it's Wednesday; a Bible study that encourages all the questions you thought you weren't allowed to ask, complete with compelling answers as dynamic as, well, Wednesday; and a grand old, southern house named for somebody called, of course, "Lydia." Does this sound exciting, yet? Ah, but it is! Dean rubs these unlikely things together with heart and depth and art and brings us to glorious life."

—The Rev. Gary Barker, Rector, Kingston Parish, Mathews, VA

Looking for Lydia; Looking for God
by Dean Robertson

ISBN   978-1-63393-100-8

Published by

 köehlerbooks™

210 60th Street
Virginia Beach, VA 23451
212-574-7939
www.koehlerbooks.com

 bitlit

A **$1.99 (or less)** eBook is available
with the purchase of this print book.

CLEARLY PRINT YOUR NAME ABOVE IN UPPER CASE

Instructions to claim your eBook edition:
1. Download the BitLit app for Android or iOS
2. Write your name in UPPER CASE on the line
3. Use the BitLit app to submit a photo
4. Download your eBook to any device

Looking for Lydia; Looking for God

From 2014 to The Civil War,
The Journey of
Thirteen Women

Dean Robertson

VIRGINIA BEACH
CAPE CHARLES

Author's note

Only a small number of women, who participated for a year or more in the Bible Study at the Lydia Roper Home, have been included in this book. Most of their names and some details have been changed to insure their privacy. At their request, Nan, Catherine, Evelyn, Terry, and Carmen have retained their real names.

Dedication

To the brave women in the Bible Study:
Thank you for your time, your trust, and your friendship.

To Albert Lonsdale Roper, Molly Roper Jenkins,
and Bruce Forsberg:
Thank you for sharing Lydia and yourselves.

To my son, Marcus Robertson Pollard,
and his wife, Paige Lindgren Weiss Pollard:
Thank you for making it all possible.

Contents

"What's past is prologue"
("The Tempest," Act 2, sc.1, l. 252)

"Abraham was the father of Isaac, and Isaac the father of Jacob ... and Boaz the father of Obed ... and Obed the father of Jesse, and Jesse the father of King David ...

And David was the father of Solomon by the wife of Uriah ... and Jacob the father of Joseph the husband of Mary, of whom Jesus was born, who is called the Messiah"
(Matthew 1:2-17).

Windsor Manor Co-ops
Spring 2014

Lydia Roper Home
Spring 2014

Prologue

IT IS A WEDNESDAY morning in April of 2014, and I am looking out my windows, old casements in a 1928 building in an urban neighborhood in Norfolk, Virginia, waiting for a door-to-door car service provided by the area's public bus company. If I'm paying attention and see her coming, my driver will pull up just as I walk out my front door, and we'll begin the fifteen-minute drive to another ninety-year-old building, which, since its construction in 1920, has been a home for elderly women and where I have spent one morning a week for more than a year talking about the Bible with a group of women in their ninth and tenth decades.

My story starts here in this building. It is the story of a miracle, although not one of those miracles where statues weep and holy faces appear in tacos. It is not a study of the Bible, nor a story about the study of the Bible; it is not a story about a small group of women; it is not a story about an unusual assisted living facility; not a history of the man who built it nor a portrait of his wife, who inspired it; it is not my own story. This is the tale of what happened when all those stories converged in the late Winter of 2013 in the residents' living room, in a large Colonial Revival building, in a bustling port city on the coast of southern Virginia.

Everything begins with the women: Kate and Neal; Inez, Evelyn and Terry; Lucille and Nan; Catherine and Wilma and Cora Mae. On two Wednesdays, Carmen was with us. Eventually, there would be Lydia.

⚜✦⚜

When I arrived at the Lydia Roper Home in February of 2013, I was a resident, not a volunteer. I had spent a year paralyzed by depression and struggling with neurological disorders; soon after Christmas I had a terrible fall. I ended up in the hospital, in a rehabilitation center and, finally, at the Roper Home. I walked up the steps of that old mansion, and I didn't come out of my room for a month. When I finally emerged, I didn't talk to anyone at my table at meals and I refused to sign up for bingo, board games, arts and crafts, or songfests. I asked if, instead of joining an activity, I could lead one. I suggested a Bible Study. The Activities Director checked with the residents. The residents said yes, and we gathered. There were four of us: Kate, Inez, Evelyn, and I.

At first, I was the only one who said a word. I lectured; eventually I created introductory outlines: probable author and date of composition; intended audience; historical context. I identified main ideas, events, and characters. When I realized it wasn't easy for some of the women to follow me in their Bibles, I typed pages of passages from the text. I typed in 22-point font. The few women who were then coming to the classes told me they were keeping the handouts, sometimes reading them later. I wrote them more thoughtfully, paid more attention to the details, tried to figure out what I wanted these pieces of paper to accomplish. I was working harder. I needed to work harder. I had found a way to survive.

By the time we started Luke's Gospel more than a year had passed and we were an even dozen. I had moved by then into my co-op in the old downtown building with its long windows opening on the neighborhood. We had just spent a few months talking about Mark, the first Gospel written, and Matthew, nearly half again as long. We were talking about Jesus, of course. But in March of 2013, when we first met in the large first floor living room, we weren't talking about Jesus at all. We started with Adam and Eve.

Before I retired from my final teaching post, I taught a course I called the Hebrew Bible as Literature. I taught that course in the independent secondary schools that were my meat and bread, in small colleges, in church adult education classes, in nursing homes, senior centers, even for a few months in a home for the blind. I once had a grant that financed classes in Women in the Hebrew Bible for a group of low-income women in Louisville, Kentucky. Those classes went on for almost four years. When they were finally over, the women who had been participating the longest took me for a day at the races at Churchill Downs. We stayed in touch for many years.

And that was how we started at Lydia Roper; I began with what I knew. We found more questions than answers. We moved as we were moved, with very little planning ahead. Our relationship with the Scriptures and our relationships with each other were changing.

Today, on this Wednesday in the spring of 2014, I arrive just as I have for almost a year. I settle in and watch our group assemble.

Chapter One

GATHERING: WHERE WE ARE

IN JUNE OF 1921, CAPTAIN John Roper, former Union soldier and, since the end of the nineteenth century, a legendary Norfolk lumber baron, died at the age of eighty-six. A month before he died, the Lydia Roper Home was chartered, named for his wife, Lydia Hand Bowen Roper, and, according to some sources, intended as a safe haven especially for "widows of Confederate soldiers and others who had no sons to provide for them." A woman who was an administrator of the Lydia Roper Home for twenty years tells me that she heard the Home was Lydia's idea. Mrs. John Roper wanted a place for women she knew whose husbands had died and left them without enough money. She wanted her husband to help. He did.

The rambling brick building, with its shingle roof and sunny front porch, sits half a short block from a busy Norfolk street, hemmed in now by a louder world. Crepe myrtles line the sidewalk; the porch is furnished with wicker chairs and sofas and pots full of flowering plants. Visitors must ring the bell to be admitted. The large entry is carpeted in soft green; a six foot tall gold-leaf mirror hangs on one wall; the stairs rise by landings to the second and third floors. It is quiet inside.

Much later, as I realize I have embarked on a search for an unaccountably elusive Lydia Roper, I will discover that on June 7, 1865, the year he returned south after the war, Captain John Lonsdale Roper married Lydia Hand Bowen at the Columbia Avenue Methodist Episcopal Church in Philadelphia and brought her from the city of her birth to the corner of Virginia that he had already mapped and claimed as his own. The 1865 membership roster for the Columbia Avenue Methodist Episcopal Church includes neither Bowens nor Ropers.

Whatever their church affiliation in Philadelphia, John and Lydia were soon established as active members of the Granby Methodist Episcopal Church in Norfolk—later Epworth United Methodist, relocated to Freemason Street. Ultimately, the Roper family would prove a strong force for Methodism in the Virginia United Methodist Church. Captain Roper's grandson Albert, three-term mayor of Norfolk, founded the Wesleymen, a men's prayer and Bible study group, which celebrated its one hundredth birthday in 2014. It still meets every Sunday morning at nine-thirty. In 1965, the Mayor published a book titled *Did Jesus Rise From the Dead: A Lawyer Looks at the Evidence* (Grand Rapids: Zondervan Publishing House, 1965). Today there are no Ropers in the congregation at Epworth United Methodist Church.

As I consider that I might want to know more about Lydia, it doesn't occur to me that there could be problems finding what seems such obvious information. I have not really moved beyond a strong imperative to write about the Bible Study and the women who come every week. I have not yet become a researcher.

However, I am curious. I begin, tentatively, with little real investment of time or attention, to look for Lydia.

I know so far that Lydia Roper bore the Captain six children and that she died in 1930 at the age of ninety. Her interment card at Elmwood Cemetery reads, simply, "cardiac failure." Lydia's heart stopped beating.

In 1963, the Roper family donated the Lydia Roper Home to the Virginia Conference of the Methodist Church; with that gift came an endowment for the maintenance of the building. A plaque in the foyer tells visitors that sometime between the Captain's death in 1921 and her own in 1930, Lydia Roper endowed the Home again.

One condition was attached to the original gift—that it retain the name of Lydia Roper.

⁂

Kate arrives a little late from her weekly hair appointment. Her hair, as always, is shiny clean and in one of those careful styles that looks like no style at all. She is classic and dressed in the way I have come to expect: slim black slacks, a long-sleeved pullover in off-white, a simple red silk scarf tied loosely at the neck. She wears small gold earrings, and I ask about her bracelet, red enamel with intricate gold insets. It was a gift from her grandchildren, who live now in Italy. When she reaches for something on the table, her sleeve is pulled back slightly. There is an intimate glimpse of pale skin, marked with the spots and prominent veins of old age. The wrist, feminine and beautiful, catches the eye. Kate's birthday is next month; she will be ninety-seven.

Today we confront what we learn is called a Portable Public Address System, acquired when I realized that too many of the women were just not able to hear me unless I shouted. Sometimes we take a break from our studies—to swap stories, to sit on the porch, to talk about the relief of not having to wear girdles or shave our legs. Today it's the P.A. system.

We play musical chairs. Kate and Evelyn and Catherine move around the room, trying out the best positions near the speaker. They are our test cases, since they are in most need of the amplified sound. I move furniture and check out the speaker in different locations. I turn the volume up, turn the volume down, adjust levels of this and that, and I think we're a success. Evelyn actually asks me to lower my voice!

When I lived here, Evelyn and I shared a table in the dining room; we still do on those Wednesdays I'm able to stay for lunch. She is a shy woman, self-effacing and kind. If someone asks for an extra dessert, Evelyn is likely to pass hers over. I was delighted to find that she has an impressive collection of large, bright, dangling earrings and that she is meticulous in her choice for each day. This week, Evelyn took me to her room to see those earrings, jumbled together in small jewelry boxes: three silver teardrops, one inside another; tiny round bouquets of enameled flowers; large silver discs from which swing ten small mother-of-pearl coins; pair after pair of gold and silver hoops. My favorite is a pair of outrageously large green enamel triangles.

We have been talking about her visiting my home since before I moved out of Lydia Roper last October. We promised each other that she would be my first guest, but circumstances of health and family have kept that from happening. Now her eyesight is failing and I worry we won't pull it off. Today's earrings are gold, circles within circles. Evelyn is ninety-three.

This room where we meet is just right for us. It's small and cozy and the furniture—two overstuffed armchairs and a small sofa covered in Williamsburg blue—provides almost a sense of luxury. I remember when all the new furniture arrived and the old, worn sets began to disappear everywhere: from the downstairs living room, from the dining room, and from the landings and corridors.

A few months ago, in a reshuffling of the activities schedule, our Bible Study was moved from the main living room to this much smaller second floor parlor with its comfortable blue furniture. We've decided that being closer together is good for practical things, like hearing each other better. It has also created a little island where we're just crowded enough to be pushed into closeness in other ways.

I'm looking it over now, as Nan distributes the handouts for our final look at the introductory material for Luke's Gospel. I take a breath and watch Nan, as she moves around the room. I watch the ladies, landed happily and willy-nilly on the perches of their choice, chatting easily with each other and with me, looking up occasionally to see if we're ready to begin. No one's in a hurry; we're perfectly at ease just being here. I am finally choosing my own perch. I usually squeeze in on the sofa with one or two residents or take an armchair. I have to be where everyone can see and hear me fairly well. Today I'm aware of the speaker on the table and of keeping my mouth close to the tiny microphone. I can hear the sound fade if I turn my head. It requires a bit more attention but I can tell the difference.

We have already worked our way through most of the Introduction to Luke's Gospel, and have talked about the basics.

Today is an easy catch-up and gives us time for a few new ideas. An important characteristic of this Gospel is the sheer number and variety of women. It is the only place where we get a glimpse of the young girl, Mary, as she hears the announcement that will change her life. It is, in fact, the only Gospel in which the Annunciation is even made to Mary. Mark doesn't include the birth narrative at all; Matthew's angel announces the event to Joseph; John's Jesus is, simply, "the Word."

Luke's story begins with a familiar greeting, "Do not be afraid." But here is Mary, a real girl, who is "perplexed by his words and ponders what sort of greeting this might be." She dares to question, "How can this be since I am a virgin?" Can she possibly, in that blinding moment, understand the angel's words? "You will conceive in your womb and bear a son, and you will name him Jesus. He will be great ... " (1:31-32).

She is very young here, on the pages of the third Gospel. Luke tells us that "Mary treasured all these words and pondered them in her heart." I will discover that it was almost easier to find Mary than it will be to find Lydia Roper, the woman for whom this old brick building is named. Here in Luke's Gospel, Mary has a story, and stories make sense of things. It will not be so easy to find stories about Lydia Roper.

Not so easy as in Luke's Gospel, where more women than Mary have their stories. Mary visits her elderly cousin Elizabeth who will give birth to the Baptist. They wait together (1:39-56).

Anna the prophetess recognizes the infant Jesus (2:36-38); the unnamed woman with the alabaster jar enters the house where Jesus is dining with a Pharisee and washes his feet with her tears (7:36-50); the wealthy women of the countryside travel with Jesus and the disciples, support them, and stay with them all the way to the cross (8:1-3; 23:55-56).

The Lydia Roper ladies seem a little surprised by this impressive parade. Inez recalls the disciples who were, by contrast, confused by Jesus' predictions of the approaching ordeal, fled when he was arrested, and failed to recognize him when he returned. Peter denied Jesus three times; later Jesus called him "the rock on which I will build my church." Nan wonders what we are supposed to take away from this. Peter is forgiven; Peter is more than forgiven. Peter is promoted! The women seem to understand from the start, yet no rewards for them.

Terry, a friend of Nan's who has been coming to the Bible Study for several weeks, asks how we're going to define "rewards."

Once again, we have questions rather than answers. We're getting accustomed to it. The questions we ask today will come up again when we read the Parable of the Prodigal Son. How do we feel about second chances, about forgiveness? How do we feel, especially, when the second chances come to someone else?

Chapter Two

GATHERING: SETTLING IN

SOME MORNINGS, I DON'T find anyone in our upstairs room and so begin a kind of treasure hunt, checking the living room, where I usually can collect Lucille and Wilma, sometimes Neal, from in front of the large flat-screen television. Kate and Inez are already heading out of their first floor rooms, on their way to the elevator. After that, I look for anyone who might have lingered in the dining room after breakfast, call into the common bathrooms, and then begin my climb to the second and third floors.

Evelyn and Nan are on the third floor, and I knock on each door. For these two women, the Bible Study has been transformative. I think, perhaps, it has been that for all of us. I have watched Evelyn risk relationships in a way she clearly hasn't before; withdrawn and often silent, she has started chatting with me and with the other women, asking questions about the Scriptures, sometimes laughing out loud. Nan has seemed stylish and confident. As the months have passed, when we were both residents and during this year as I have traveled to the Lydia Roper Home, Nan and I have become friends. We laugh, we talk about our lives and our husbands, we watch movies, we let down our guard. I think these years at the Lydia Roper Home have been about women of a certain age building a community of trust and affection. I think, in fact, they have been about love.

⚜

We're finally all here, only a few minutes behind schedule, choosing seats, settling down, settling in, still chatting about our week since last Wednesday. We're ready to begin with a question Kate asked two weeks ago. Kate, however, is sitting in the hall. Of all possible Wednesdays, the hair dresser is late, and Kate has been left waiting. We shuffle papers, begin half-heartedly, try to stall; it hardly seems fair that Kate miss the discussion. And she arrives.

Kate, who was one of the pioneers in this Bible Study, was too reserved to speak at all for months. Today, she is best known among us for her provocative questions. Today's question is typical, the kind I'm hearing more from everyone. It's a difficult question that makes me think, a question I haven't heard before, a question that might not have an answer.

"What do you feel, as a Gentile, about Jesus' exclusion of Gentiles from his ministry?"

We begin: First I point out that Jesus didn't preach to Gentiles, but he hung out with them. We look at stories like the one in which he meets the Samaritan woman at the well (John 4:4-42); or his controversial dinner at the home of a Pharisee when a Gentile woman, a "sinner," washes his feet with her hair, and has her sins forgiven (Luke 7:36-50).

Sometimes, when we are ambushed by something like this, an unnamed woman letting down her hair, we are quiet.

I notice Neal, with her slow eyes that can seem sleepy. I used to worry that she just wasn't listening; I was wrong. Today, as usual, she doesn't talk; hearing is a way of participating, too. Someone remembers the Parable of the Good Samaritan (Luke 10:25-37). My own favorite story about Jesus and a Gentile is in Mark 7:26-30. A woman comes to Jesus asking that he cast out a demon from her young daughter. Jesus refuses because she is "a Gentile, of Syrophoenician origin" and he tells her that the Jews (the "children") must not have their "food" given to the Gentiles (the "dogs"). She confronts him and insists that "even the dogs under the table eat the children's crumbs." Jesus, who so far has not looked too good in this story, considers and relents. He tells her that, "for saying that, you may go; the demon has left your daughter."

Jesus and the Gentiles. There is nothing in the Gospels to suggest that Jesus had any interest in preaching to anyone but his fellow Jews, but Luke's Jesus is passionately interested in helping anyone who needs help. He "went around doing good" (Acts 10:38).

We have reached a good resolution to Kate's question, and we're ready for our handouts: twelve pages of passages from Luke's Gospel. Nan has them in hand. Ever since Nan arrived at Lydia Roper, I've had an assistant. Without ever being asked, she has simply taken over the job of passing out papers and, if necessary, collecting them when we've finished for the day. Even on the days when she's in pain, she shows up. Today she looks like she looked to me on the day she arrived—an oasis. Nan has achieved something I apparently cannot. In her casually stylish slacks and blouses, she is one of those women I used to refer to with envy as "pulled together." She just turned eighty-six, nearly twenty years my senior, but Nan is in better shape than I was at fifty. She still sits by her daughter's swimming pool in a bathing suit.

⚜

Passages from Luke in front of us, we wade in; I read one out loud, pose a question or two, then we wait through the inevitable few minutes of silence. On this Wednesday, we find we are tired and can't quite think of what we want to say. Wilma comes in late and is crying. She has wrapped herself in a blanket covered with bright sailboats. She is quiet, but the tears continue; she looks young.

The new amplifier is already set up facing the room, so we push on. I am able to turn on the small transmitter, drop it into my T-shirt pocket, and clip the microphone to my collar. It falls off a few times, but I'm getting the hang of it. We laugh, and Wilma smiles at me.

While the ladies think, I remember that the week after Easter I wanted to find some kind of key to sum up and compare the three Synoptic Gospels, just to be sure we could see that, while they all tell the same basic story, they tell it in very personal ways.

I looked online for one of those charts that lists all the parables and shows which Gospels do and don't include them. Aside from being, frankly, boring, they all were printed in type so small that no one over forty would even be able to see it on the page.

The teacher in me imagines that down the road, if we keep at it, we might occasionally manage to read a passage and say, "That's Mark!" or "That has to be one of the parables in Luke!" or "That's Matthew's angel."

Instead of Internet charts, I typed a handout of the Resurrection stories from all four Gospels, back to back, with no introduction or commentary. Mark's Gospel stops at the empty tomb; Matthew provides an earthquake, shaking guards, the women who know Jesus immediately and the disciples who doubt; Luke's Jesus is resurrected in Jerusalem and stays with the disciples for forty days; John introduces "the other disciple, the one whom Jesus loved."

In each case, when the angel announces that Jesus has risen, he opens with, "Do not be afraid." The same is true of the Annunciation stories. Jesus is coming and the angel says to Joseph, to Mary, to the shepherds, "Do not be afraid."

I raise another question that doesn't necessarily have an answer. "Why do you think the angels say that?"

Inez speaks first, "It might be like when a small child is lost in the supermarket and a guard has to come up to him to take him to his parents; the guard wants to reassure him: 'Don't be afraid.'"

Terry thinks that maybe these people just weren't accustomed to angels at the door and were frightened by what they saw.

I pointed out that sometimes "it is a fearful thing to fall into the hands of the living God" (Hebrews 10:31) and that it could be a kind of notice of the life-changing encounter that was about to occur. "Don't be afraid," even though something bigger and scarier than an angel is about to happen to you.

We remember the Old Testament stories about coming face-to-face with the Divine: Jacob's wounded hip; Moses' shining face. "It is a fearful thing. Do not be afraid." And so, inevitably, we wander from our main topic, wade into deeper waters, get, perhaps, a little afraid ourselves, and are consoled by the palpable sense of keeping company together in this small room, curled up on couches and in armchairs.

Wilma, always cold and a little confused, is wrapped in her blanket. We spend time with ourselves, with each other, with the Bible. We escape, for a couple of hours a week, the sometimes harsh realities of daily life, of loneliness, age, poor health, fading memories, limited mobility, the terrible emptiness of not enough to do. At the end of John's Gospel, Jesus says to Peter, "Very truly, I tell you, when you were younger, you used to fasten your own belt and to go wherever you wished. But when you grow old, you will stretch out your hands, and someone else will fasten a belt around you and take you where you do not wish to go" (21:18).

I hung around for a long time that day in the week after the Resurrection.

❦

It is still Wednesday at Lydia Roper, and Nan has handed out the passages from Luke's Gospel:

"There was a man who had two sons. The younger of them said to his father, 'Father, give me the share of the property that will belong to me.' So he divided his property between them. A few days later the younger son gathered all he had and traveled to a distant country, and there he squandered his property in dissolute living ... When he came to himself he said, 'How many of my father's hired hands have bread enough and to spare, but here I am dying of hunger! I will get up and go to my father, and I will say to him, 'Father, I have sinned against heaven and before you; I am no longer worthy to be called your son ... ' while he was still far off, his father saw him and was filled with compassion; he ran and put his arms around him and kissed him ... the father said to his slaves, 'Quickly, bring out a robe—the best one—and put it on him; put a ring on his finger and sandals on his feet ... for this son of mine was dead and is alive again; he was lost and is found.

"Now the elder son was in the field; and when he came and approached the house, he heard music and dancing. He called one of the slaves and asked what was going on. He replied, 'Your brother has come, and your father has killed the fatted calf, because he has got him back safe and sound.' Then he became angry and refused to go in. His father came out and began to plead with him. But he answered his father, 'Listen! For all these years I have been working like a slave for you, and I have never disobeyed your command; yet you have never given me even a young goat so that I might celebrate with my friends. But when this son of yours came back, who has devoured your property with prostitutes, you killed the fatted calf for him! Then the father said to him, 'Son, you are always with me, and all that is mine is yours. But we had to celebrate and rejoice because this brother of yours was dead and has come to life; he was lost and has been found'" (Luke 15:11-32).

We had already explored the nature of parables when we read Matthew's Gospel, but we talk about it again today. Since Luke's Gospel has many more parables than the other two, we feel the need for a quick reminder of what we're doing. In a book called *Why Jesus?,* William H. Willimon suggests that the parables are like mirrors in which we see ourselves more clearly (28). He suspects that Jesus tells parables, not to explain his message or to "pass out the right answers" (27). What Jesus really wants is for us to dig more deeply for the right questions and, when we find them, ask them fearlessly. Maybe "Jesus tells these stories in order to make you a character in the story, in order to put your life in the grand narrative of God's salvation of the world" (29).

No longer asking what the Parable of the Prodigal Son means, but rather listening for what it might be asking us about ourselves, I read it aloud a second time, and our questions are, instead, "Where am I in this story? In what ways have I been prodigal? What does *prodigal* even mean? Can I imagine myself as the younger son, the older son, the father? If I do that, what might I learn that is different from an answer to, "What does this Parable mean?"

We set even those questions aside for a while and just talk about the parable as a story: What disturbs? What comforts? What surprises? Do we like it? This last is not a question we often allow ourselves to ask about the Bible. *Do we like it?*

Kate, it turns out, doesn't like this parable much at all. "Is this just telling us that we can go out and do whatever bad things we want and it's all right?"

In Matthew's Gospel, Jesus says we are to be forgiven, and forgiven again, "not seven, but seventy times seven" (Matt 18:22). Matthew's Jesus tells us, of course, that we also have to forgive just that extravagantly.

Today we want to escape from home with the younger son, who asked for his inheritance and, seeking freedom or adventure, "travelled to a distant country and ... squandered his property"; to stand with the older brother who has stayed at home, "working like a slave," never disobeying; to mourn with the father for the loss of his son; to rely, with the father, on the son who is "always with" him; to panic and to scheme with the prodigal, as he convinces himself he is "dying of hunger" and plots his appeal to his father, "I have sinned against heaven and before you;" to resent, with the older son, the unfairness of a fatted calf for his brother while his father has "never even given me a young goat that I might celebrate with my friends." And, finally, to share with the father the moment when he recognizes his son "while he was still far off." The Scripture at that point describes the father's emotion as "compassion," but I have always experienced that moment when he sees his lost son, walking toward him, still at a distance, as one of pure joy. Is that how we get to compassion, through joy? The ladies ask question after question; they are hungry for the talk today.

I remember that someone says, "The father is just happy to have his son back!" As if that settles it; the father is happy and so he forgives.

Neal, who doesn't talk, who lowers those beautiful eyelids and listens, says, "I know just how that older son feels. I was the good one, and everyone always loved my sister best." But Neal is sitting here, with her history as the "older brother," and she can say to us, "Time fixes everything. That prodigal son will change; that older brother will forgive him." Neal has grown into hope. And, with my own hope, I listen in amazement as she talks and talks and talks.

Something good is happening this morning in Lydia Roper's house.

The Prodigal Son
(Luke 15:11-32)

We read the Parable of The Woman with the Alabaster Jar (Luke 7: 36-50), who walks alone into a dinner party at the home of a Pharisee, carrying a jar of perfumed ointment. Kate points out that the ointment would have been expensive. The woman is a prostitute; she's spent her profits from the sale of her body for salve to anoint Jesus. We talk about how much guts it took to walk into this houseful of prominent religious men, who would have known exactly what she was, and to wash Jesus' feet "with her tears," and "dry them with her hair" (Luke 7: 36-50).

Terry says without hesitation, "The woman was courageous because she wanted Jesus so badly she was willing to do anything."

But Neal's experience is that "when we're doing something really hard, when we're so afraid, we just kind of go into a trance, don't even see our surroundings anymore."

For a few minutes, surrounded by our small room in the Lydia Roper Home, we close our eyes and sit in that room in first century Palestine and visualize this "woman in the city who was a sinner."

The Anointing of Jesus
(Matthew 26:1-16)

I hope we can all see her now. How old is she, how tall or short, thin or heavy, wearing what clothes? I read again that "she stood behind him at his feet, weeping, and began to bathe his feet with her tears and to dry them with her hair." Why is she crying? We've met her before, of course, when we were talking about Kate's question and Jesus' relationship with the Gentiles.

We reconsider the stories of two sinners, a prodigal son and a prostitute. We have been there; we know these people. For which one do we feel instinctive sympathy? For which one, something more conditional? There's not a right answer here. We've discovered by now that there rarely is.

We've almost run out of time, so we'll take this careless young wastrel and this bold prostitute with us into our afternoons. We will think about them, whether we plan to or not. Sometimes leaving questions hanging is the very best answer.

Before we leave, we read a very short section of the passage about Mary's visit to Elizabeth and Elizabeth's spontaneous prayer, "Blessed are you among women and blessed is the fruit of your womb, Jesus..." (1:42). Inez and Nan identify that right away as the "Hail Mary," or the "Ave Maria."

Inez was born in a small town further south whose population according to the 2010 census is under 5000. It is nestled in a valley between a mountain range to the east and a plateau to the west. Inez worked in the health profession from an early age. Eventually, she came to Norfolk for a visit, and she met Dave. They were married for nearly two decades. Her great loss came when Dave died from a brain tumor that remained undiagnosed until surgery was impossible. By then, Inez had grown accustomed to her life in Norfolk. Offered a job, she accepted.

We talk about prayer; we talk about meditation. Someone says she has heard the Rosary and is put off that it "just repeats the same things over and over and over." So I ask what value there might be in that kind of repetition.

Inez says, "It just relaxes you."

The reflective approach we are taking to these parables is not new; we are firmly grounded in centuries-old Christian tradition. In the sixteenth century, Ignatius Loyola, son of a wealthy Castilian family, at an early age a knight, a soldier, and a diplomat, suffered a severe wound in battle. During a long period of convalescence, he read a book on the lives of the saints and a life of Christ. Moved by this reading, he withdrew to fast and pray and to engage in the more drastic practice of scourging. An immediate result of this was a profound religious experience after which he began to write down the notes for what would become his great life's work, *The Spiritual Exercises*. It is from Loyola's *Spiritual Exercises* that we are drawing the idea of imagining ourselves inside the Gospel stories. What we are doing is called Ignatian Reflection. Instructions for beginning these exercises usually start with some version of, "Close your eyes and breathe deeply until you are relaxed and calm." So Inez is on the mark in her understanding of at least one of the values of meditation. It just relaxes you.

We can't seem to let go today. We talk about receiving; we talk about receiving forgiveness. What does receiving forgiveness do to you? Why is it often harder to accept forgiveness than to offer it? Why does Jesus say, of the woman: "I tell you her sins, which were many, have been forgiven; hence she has shown great love.

But the one to whom little is forgiven, loves little."

What can that mean? This question trails after the ladies as Nan collects papers for one more week of passages from Luke, and we walk out the door. We'll come back to this a week from now.

⚜

I arrive early and make it in time for breakfast. I take my old seat at the table with Evelyn; after breakfast I move to the table that Kate and Inez share, and we talk about the start of this Bible Study, trying to remember who was there in those early gatherings. We're sure of Kate, Inez, and Evelyn. We don't know if there were others.

This reminiscing opens the doors between us in a new way. We have a history. We have become good friends.

We now look for opportunities to talk outside our Bible Study. This morning, I walk upstairs to pull out my laptop and make some notes for this afternoon. Neal is already there, and I join her. We wander into a conversation about how it feels to lose your memory. Neal used to keep all the books for her dad on a farm south of here: cotton, corn, peanuts, tobacco. Siblings all dead now, and Neal can't remember the name of the town where she grew up.

She talks about her old bike, one she's had since she was fourteen; she believes it's in a neighbor's garage, in good shape. The bike is red, and she won't let her young grandson ride it. "He'd have it about twenty minutes!" New ones just fall apart. Neal claims she could ride that bike "anyway you could think of—backwards or standing up." Now that's an image for a meditation! Our talk is slow, comfortable, rambling.

I try to describe growing up in the North Georgia woods. We talk about our mothers. Neal says when her mother died no one would tell her where she was buried because they were afraid she would get too upset and "try to dig her up. And I might have done it!" It's not clear when all this happened.

Today Nan is in obvious pain and having trouble breathing. Over the weekend, Wilma was taken to the hospital and will almost certainly go from there to a nursing home. I don't let myself think much about the ages and the increasing fragility of these women I have come to love.

The Woman with the Alabaster Jar. I read the story aloud for the third time.

Five minutes for imagining. We have already determined that given her time and place, in first century Palestine, she would have been dark-skinned, with black hair and dark eyes. We can see those eyes flashing, even in her moment of vulnerability. It takes some spirit to be there at all.

Nan speaks up confidently: "She is tall and thin and beautiful."

Neal adds, "She looks strong; she's healthy and she's brave."

Terry insists that she's "not too young; she's been a sinner for a while." We agree. We can almost see her.

But why is this woman "weeping"?

Neal thinks she's crying because she doesn't want to be there; Terry says she is aware of her sins and, unlike the other men she has known, Jesus is kind and accepting. Kate thinks she's crying because she's relieved: she has finally been forgiven.

"I tell you her sins, which were many, have been forgiven; hence she has shown great love. But the one to whom little is forgiven, loves little."

We ask our question again. What does that mean?

Terry: "So if someone has done bad things, too, it's easier for her to understand us, or the other way around. If I've sinned, I can understand your sins."

I tell them about Isaiah's Suffering Servant by whose "wounds we are healed" (Isaiah 53:5) and the concept of the "wounded healer" taken from Greek mythology.

"By his wounds, we are healed." What does that mean? Silence, until Kate says, "I think that's part of the mystery; we can't understand it. We just accept it on faith."

Who is the wounded healer in all the Gospel stories? Everyone is smiling; no one quite speaks up. Both Nan and Terry whisper "Jesus."

We make the shift between these two sinners one more time as we reread the parable of the two sons.

What does *prodigal* mean? What do you think first when you hear the name of this parable, The Prodigal Son? The answers include greedy, wasteful, irresponsible: someone who runs away.

At home, I have looked up the definition of *prodigal*.

1. Spending money or resources freely and recklessly; wastefully extravagant. Synonyms: wasteful, extravagant, spendthrift; improvident; imprudent

2. Having or giving something on a lavish scale. Synonyms: generous; liberal; unsparing; bounteous.

I read the two definitions. After a few minutes of silence, I pose the questions: "Is the younger son the only prodigal character in this story? If we use the second definition, who is the most prodigal of all, right from the start?"

We all get it: the father, of course. Perhaps his most prodigal act is handing over the money and letting the boy go, although he is obviously, outrageously prodigal when he takes him back, no blame, no demands, just acceptance, love, gratitude, and generosity.

Now we ask ourselves: *How am I prodigal? Am I prodigal enough?*

Someone says that I'm prodigal in coming to do the Bible Study every week; I have to confess I do it because I like it. Maybe I'm prodigal in just how much I do like it.

Terry has been quiet today, but on our way out we have time to sit down while she thinks a minute, then says, "Those two definitions have just changed the way I think about that whole story."

About once a month, Terry and Nan and I go back to my place to watch a movie and treat ourselves to a pizza—with everything. When I lived at Lydia Roper, Nan often came to my room and we would spend whole days doing nothing but watching movies, missing heaven-knows-what scheduled activities. When I left, we decided to keep up the tradition. Every month, when I see her out in the world like that, I am aware that Nan is a little weaker, tires more easily, needs her inhaler more often. I am aware of her eighty-six years.

Twice married, the second time a love story. When her

husband was in the final stages of cancer, her daughter, Diane, drove to their home in Florida, packed them up, and moved them to Chesapeake to live with her. Nan's Jerry died two months later, and she stayed with Diane for three years. In 2013, mother and daughter made the hard decision that Nan would move to the Lydia Roper Home. They were concerned that she was spending so much time alone, that she sometimes confused her medications, that she had forgotten to turn the stove off, that she was too dependent on Diane. They agreed that she needed the company of people her own age. Diane was afraid the situation was damaging their relationship. Nan says Diane was becoming the mother, she, the child, and that it wasn't good. And so she appeared one day, in the front hall of the Roper Home, looking just like herself, smiling tentatively, as uncertain as I was on my first day, and clear salvation for me.

I am glad she walked in that door.

This morning Nan says, "Now I believe God wanted me here; there are some people I can help." I tell her I think so, too, and I remind her again how much she helped me, by just arriving. There's something about Nan that makes you believe there might still be possibilities.

We turn to our summary of the Synoptic Gospels. We see we've covered a lot of ground since the first of the year. It's a good moment. Before I can even get started, Kate clears her throat.

"Before we stop talking about Luke, I'd like to know if he was really a doctor." I have to say I don't know, but I believe the scholarly position generally is that he very well might have been. I talk a bit about what doctors did in first century Palestine. I will need to do more reading.

I make some introductory comments about Acts, the story of the early church.

After a short break, I move from Luke's Gospel to his second volume, the Acts of the Apostles. It was years before someone told me that Luke's Gospel and Acts are really a large two-volume work. Acts follows the early years of the church from Jerusalem to the far reaches of Paul's missionary journeys. We will meet Peter again and James, the brother of Jesus, who shepherd the young Jewish members of the movement in Jerusalem. We will learn that Peter, rather than Paul, is first in extending the gospel to the Gentiles. We will get to know Saul, more commonly Paul, before and after his meeting with the risen Christ on the road to Damascus. We will watch him set out across the countryside on his mission to the Gentiles. We will come to understand that the ascension of Jesus into heaven, while an end to his ministry on earth, is the beginning of the life of the church as the Apostles set out from Jerusalem.

Today, though, we just take a deep breath and relax with the feeling of having, once again, accomplished something pretty big. Finishing up a project like the Synoptics is fulfilling, but the buzz of excitement around us comes from knowing we'll be at this again in two weeks; it is work we have come to love.

We leave with an assignment. Anticipating that we might not have time today to join the two apostles and Jesus on the road to Emmaus, I printed an exercise in Ignatian prayer that allows us to say our final goodbye to Luke's Gospel at home. In the upper right-hand corner is an endearing sketch of a rather confused looking monk in a long brown robe (http://www.msgr. ca/msgr-3/personalitytypeprayers.html).

You are one of the two disciples on the road to Emmaus on Easter afternoon. Close your eyes after reading the Scripture passage and try to relive the whole scene from beginning to end ... invite Jesus to stay with you: 'The day is nearly over. The night is at hand. Stay with us!'"

Pilgrims on the Road to Emmaus
(Luke 24:13-25)

Everybody has questions before we start packing up, heading toward stairs and elevator reluctantly, still talking. Nan and I confer about the health of the plant she gave me; Kate, looking ahead, wants to know about Paul: did he really help at the stoning of Stephen? Neal gives me a quick hug. The ladies go in to lunch. I head to the front porch to wait for my ride.

Chapter Three

"IN THE BEGINNING ... "
HOW WE GOT HERE

AT THE LYDIA ROPER Home next week, we will begin our exploration of The Acts of the Apostles. Here, on these pages, we will leave Acts behind and waive the chance to get acquainted with Peter and with Paul. We will go, instead, back to where we started. And I will continue my increasingly urgent quest for Lydia, the woman whose story surrounds us in this house where we have spent over a year in a study of the very best stories.

By this point, I am frustrated and intrigued to discover that there is little to be found about Lydia Roper. I have the dates: birth, marriage, children, death. I have very little else. I can't quite understand it. Soon I will find myself spending hours at the library, making use of the free access to genealogy sites. I will become increasingly caught in the puzzle that is this woman's life.

The house itself is a player in the drama; its history creates possibilities. We exist in a crucible of opportunities, and in these rooms I am hopeful that one day I might really find Lydia Roper. I am in touch with her great-granddaughter, Caroline, who sings with the Welsh Choir of Southern California. This week in Norfolk I drank coffee with Lydia's great-grandson, Albert. I spent an hour on the telephone with Al's sister, Molly, in Lynchburg, Virginia. There might be photographs of that Philadelphia bride, just arrived in this city of her husband's choosing, where he would cut timber, build sawmills and railroads and canals, make his fortune and his name, and where she would lead her quiet life and fill a house with children. Records from 1893 report six children born to John and Lydia Roper. A son, John, born in 1872, died as an infant. So I know that between 1866 and 1879, Lydia grieved and gave birth. I'm not sure of much else. She still eludes me.

But long before I went in search of Lydia, the ladies and I made our beginning. In March of 2013 I introduced this Bible Study at the Lydia Roper Home with what I knew and could talk about easily—the Hebrew Bible. I wasn't in very good shape and mostly I wanted something to do that would occupy my mind and take it off my circumstances. I wanted something to do that wouldn't be much of a challenge; my confidence was low. But I knew one thing. For me, work is consolation and survival. If I were going to get through without losing my mind, I had to find a way to work again, and my work is reading and teaching. I spent over thirty years with Shakespeare and Eliot, with Faulkner and Dickinson and Hawthorne, thirty years with Hamlet and Ophelia, Dorothea Brooke and Hester Prynne; almost thirty with the Bible.

When I was in graduate school, a woman named Mary Rich first taught me to read the Bible as literature. I learned the thing that was to shape my life for the next few decades: this old, familiar text is new, and bottomless. No matter how—or how often—I read it, I will never be through with it. When Mary retired, she shipped from Mill Valley, California, to my home in Louisville, Kentucky, ten large cartons that contained her entire theology library. Those books were the foundation for the course that would eventually become my own. When I left Louisville, they moved with me, and moved with me, then moved with me again. They overflowed floor-to-ceiling bookcases in Kentucky and Michigan and Virginia. When I retired, I gave most of them to the young man to whom I entrusted The Hebrew Bible as Literature. It felt like exactly the right thing to do. Most days I miss them.

There are books in our room at the Lydia Roper Home. We

are flanked on two entire walls by built-in bookcases. They hold, among other things: Dorothy L. Sayers' Lord Peter Wimsey mysteries; *Reader's Digest Condensed Books*; an old set of *World Book Encyclopedias*; assorted novels by Danielle Steele, James Patterson, and Janet Evanovich; video cassettes of "A Fine Romance," starring Judy Dench and a PBS series of Peter Wimsey stories. They also contain, oddly, single volumes like *The Green Gauntlet* by R.F. Delderfield (1968) and *Adventures in Friendship*, written in 1910 by David Grayson. Stacked neatly on one shelf are boxes of Checkers and Scrabble.

I remember Mrs. Grantly, who lived at Lydia Roper while I was there, always carrying a paperback mystery with her. She was never without one. We never discussed them, and I wasn't sure that she read them. When I came into the dining room, Mrs. Grantly smiled and saluted, book in hand. She left sometime in the Winter.

Franz Kafka once wrote that "a book must be the axe for the frozen sea within us." I didn't know it at that moment, in the living room at the Lydia Roper Home, but I was badly in need of an axe.

❧❧

In the 1980's, I spent several years in churches, in senior centers, in grant-sponsored workshops, offering a course I called Women in the Hebrew Bible. I thought that since here at the Roper Home we were a group of women together, in a place named for a woman, it made sense to try that. It also provided me with a clear focus and a way of limiting and, if I needed to, ending things. I could pick a few stories and see how it went. I wasn't at all sure I could hold up. I wasn't at all sure anyone would be interested. But we made our beginning, the women of the Lydia Roper Home, the women of the Bible, and I.

Naturally, we started with Eve. I had no handouts. I still had my notes and outlines from my years of teaching, but they would have to be completely reworked. In looking back through my files from those first few months, I see that the first of the outlines for the Lydia Roper ladies appeared with our study of Sarah, and even then I provided no introductory information, just a summary of the story and the main ideas. Eventually, there were handouts on some of the most intriguing women: Bathsheba; Rahab, the prostitute (Joshua 2); Ruth. The quality of the handouts gradually improved, but it was months before the best ones appeared. As with every part of this particular experience, I was learning as I went, a novice every day.

As it turns out, the willingness to be beginners was world-shifting for us all. What we did during those first months was continue to show up. The shifting of worlds came later. In early March of that year, I desultorily typed up a page of notes to get me going, mostly just a little background information about myself, my teaching experience, my own study of the Bible in graduate school in California. Remember, these women didn't know me at all. I had been there a month, had a bad attitude, had never interacted with anyone and had no intention of changing that. In the comfortable role of teacher, I could stay sane, stay separate, and hang on until I could get out of there; I figured a month or two.

That first day I think I made a few opening remarks about the women in the Bible and what I thought about them, and why they interested me. I was saying things I'd said a dozen times in a dozen different places, talking about why I wanted to talk about the Bible. I could have done it in my sleep and some days nearly did. I am always interested in the Bible, always energized by the chance to dig into a text, but I really can't say that I cared much about what was going on at that point. It was something to do, that I could do without effort, that got me out of my room once or twice a week, and by then I did at least understand the importance of getting dressed and walking downstairs. I don't think I could have told you the name of one member of that pioneer crew; now I see their faces when I close my eyes.

I came to the Lydia Roper Home sick and I left well. I arrived with no hope; I left knowing I had something to offer. I left knowing I had to come back. The ladies with whom I spend my Wednesdays have pushed open their minds and hearts to an old text, to each other, and to new ideas; they don't stop asking questions. We look for answers together. The mystery of how all that happened is really what I'm after here.

We were on the threshold of so much we couldn't have anticipated: my unexpectedly extended time at Lydia Roper;

the Bible Studies that would survive beyond my eight months' residency; that primal story of beginnings told in the first three chapters of Genesis. All our resurrections. I was there, and Kate and Inez—from the same dining room table—and my table mate, Evelyn, wearing her beautiful earrings that I hadn't yet even noticed. Was Catherine there? Was Wilma? We all seemed younger even that short time ago.

Kate has been to the hospital since then. Inez's legs swell and weaken and she has much more trouble getting around, even with her walker. Evelyn's hearing and eyesight are worse. My spinal woes don't get better. And yet in many ways we all seem years younger. I am filled with energy every week as I prepare to head to Lydia Roper then race home to write and to prepare next week's outlines and discussion.

Today nearly a dozen women are actively engaged in challenging discussions of the most important subject in the world; we are forging new friendships. I think we are happy.

After knowledge drove them out of their Garden, did Adam and Eve, too, get happy in that flawed human way we all get happy? With their "garments of skins ... sent forth ... to till the ground" (Gen. 3:21, 23), they were just at the start of their great adventure. The ladies at the Lydia Roper Home haven't come here for new adventures. They've come here, perhaps, to count out the days remembering the old ones. They've come here because they've run out of other places to go. *They've come here to die.* It took a long time sitting very still before I was able to type that. They have, in fact, come here to die. Some weeks I can hardly bear to travel to this place where, against all the odds, we are finding a new energy for living.

Margaret, Lydia Roper's oldest daughter, spent her last years at the Lydia Roper Home. She cried often, and she asked for her mother.

Tomorrow, as we approach the Acts of the Apostles in our Bible Study, I will travel early, to be there for breakfast. I'll sit for a while with Evelyn at our old table. I'll cross the room to visit with Kate and Inez. I'll hope for an empty chair next to Catherine. I'll squeeze in between Neal and Lucille. I'll make the rounds, hearing their stories, telling them tales of this week's adventures with my neighbors in the co-op.

I want to ask the pioneers about their impressions, back when we were reading the first chapters of Genesis, about their reasons for coming back, about how it has changed for them over this year and three months. And I will talk to some of the women, like Neal and Nan and Lucille, who arrived after we'd been going for a while. What did they think? What did they like? They, too, came and then came again. I'll be typing into my laptop, stopping occasionally to show to anyone who hasn't seen it a photograph of my cat, Isaac.

Kate, Neal, and Lucille have met Isaac. They came one day in the Spring to visit me in my new home. We had kept their destination a surprise, and I opened my door to an astonished Kate. They stayed for more than an hour. Neal, eyes closed, sat comfortably in the old platform rocker; Lucille looked around, smiling, asking about all my pictures; Kate and I talked about the Bible.

⚜

There are many stories about exactly how and when the Lydia Roper Home had its beginning. I read microfilm at the Sargeant Memorial Collection of local history at the Norfolk Library until my neck aches. I sit at my computer until I'm too stiff to get out of the chair. I make pleading calls to strangers at the Virginia Conference of the United Methodist Church in Richmond, to whom the Ropers gave the Roper Home in 1963; at Virginia United Methodist Homes, which now owns and manages the Home; at Randolph-Macon College, which housed the historical records before VUMH had an archive facility; at the Library of Virginia, and at Epworth United Methodist Church on Freemason Street in Norfolk, just a few blocks from where the Captain and Lydia lived. I look at Google maps and find that the street address for that residence, which was printed in Lydia's small obituary, shows an empty corner and an avenue of mature trees. The three houses Captain Roper built or bought for his children, one for George and the double-house for Virginia and Margaret, are still there. The double-house, as the family calls it, is two large houses, built in 1900, joined on the second floor, so the sisters could visit each other without going outside. Margaret was thirty-four; Virginia, only twenty-six.

322 and 324 Freeman Street
The Double-House

In 1915, Margaret Roper married, and she and her husband lived in the "outside" house, facing Dunmore Street. Virginia lived in the "inside" house until her death in 1945. In the Spring of 1946 Leighton and Molly moved into Virginia's house with their family: young Leighton was six; Albert was four; Molly was pregnant with her daughter, also Molly, who is my age. In 1966, Margaret died, at the age of one hundred, a resident of the Lydia Roper Home. In 1972, Leighton Roper died; in 1999, his wife, Molly, died. The family sold the double-house. The house that Captain John Roper purchased for himself and Lydia was demolished in 1941.

⁂

Today I am at home. I send out emails and am drowned in responses. This morning I was so caught up in a barrage of increasingly informative responses to one of my recent inquiries that I read, and answered with more questions, until well after three in the afternoon. At this point, the result is uncertainty, and all I can find is that sometime in 1920 or 1921, Captain John

Roper either "built," "established," "donated," or "founded" the Lydia Roper Home. The Home either was, or was not, intended as a haven for Confederate widows. Two sources say yes; a local historian who grew up in the area says, "The Confederate widows twist likely came about as a result of rationalizing having a *Damn Yankee* establish a very useful and needed charitable home in an extremely Confederate area. Even one hundred years after The War, partisan feelings about Northerners were still quite strong." A family member says the original charter more likely read something like, " ... for impoverished white women in the city of Norfolk."

Well.

There are two stories in the Bible about how the world began. On that first winter morning in 2013, I started with an exercise designed to help us find those stories. I read aloud Gen. 1:1-2:3, written sometime between 597-587 BCE, during or soon after the Babylonian Exile. It is poetry, probably for reading aloud in religious ceremonies. The creation is divided into six days of God's work and one sacred day of rest. It is a story with which we are all familiar. The God called *Elohim*, translated as God, speaks into the "formless void and darkness" and creates, by fiat: Day and Night; the firmament, to be called "Sky"; the Earth and the Seas; "plants yielding seed, and fruit trees of every kind"; the sun, the moon, and the stars; "every living creature ... with which the waters swarm, and every winged bird"; "the wild animals of the earth of every kind"; and, finally, "humankind in his image, in the image of God ... male and female." On the seventh day, God rests "from all the work he had done in creation." And he "blessed the seventh day and hallowed it."

The Creation of Light
(Genesis 1:3)

The Fall
(Genesis 3:1-7)

Chapter Two of Genesis, with its conclusion in Chapter Three, tells a very different kind of story. Written nearly five centuries before Chapter One, it is a primitive narrative, drawing on the folk tales of oral tradition, with a God who sculpted man with his own hands, who laid down rules and threatened death if they were broken and who walked "in the garden at the time of the evening breeze." This is a story that even has a talking serpent! The God of Chapter Two, known as *Yahweh* (the Lord), creates, in an order different than that of Chapter One: the man, from "the dust of the ground"; the garden, from which he "made to grow every tree that is pleasant to the sight and good for food"; and, "every animal of the field and every bird of the air." Only after Adam has named the animals, does Yahweh "cause a deep sleep" to fall on him, take a rib from his side, and create woman.

The most obvious discrepancy between the two stories is in the order of creation. A quick review told us that. The other variation, less easy to identify, is that of style. Chapter One is precise, incantatory, conjuring the elements of the universe with words. Its language is liturgical, its refrain, "God saw that it was good." The God of Chapter One creates from afar, by command. In Chapter Two, God is there, almost human himself, as he "forms man from the dust of the ground" and "breathes into his nostrils."

The story unfolds like a fairy tale: the owner of the Garden sets up a familiar situation, the temptation of the One Forbidden Thing. He tells the man and the woman about all that is provided for them. He describes the only thing they must not touch, and then he looks away (or does he?), the temptation left dangling. He is a God who stays involved, though—warning, threatening, seeking, questioning, cursing, and ultimately banishing his creatures because "the man has become like one of us." God is not only there; he is jealous.

With this background established, I now could concentrate on Eve. We respond even to the sound of the name: Eve, created from Adam's rib, as his "helpmate"; Eve, tempted by the serpent, eating the forbidden fruit, tempting her husband to eat; Eve, responsible for violating Eden and ushering pain and suffering into the world; Eve, the weak link. I started, again, at the beginning, and I tried to offer a different way of looking at this woman whose image has shaped our days. I started with the language of Chapter One, a story in which God says, with teasing ambiguity, "Let us make humankind in our image, according to our likeness ... " And so, "God created humankind in his image, in the image of God he created them, male and female he created them."

Do we even need to talk about what that says? "In the image of God ... male and female."

In Chapter Two, the infamous Adam's Rib story, the original Hebrew words make a difference in our understanding of the relationship of male to female. That which Yahweh molded from the dust and into which he blew the breath of life was called *adham,* a play on *adhamah,* a word which, in Hebrew, translates something like "creature of earth," a being without gender. God's first creation was neither male nor female. It was, simply, human—alive, made from the dirt of the earth and filled with God's own spirit. At the point in the story when Eve is separated from Adam's body, the Hebrew changes and, for the first time, a distinction is made. The woman is *isha,* a female; the man, *ish,* a male. They become themselves at this moment of joint creation.

I am reminded of Paul's catalogue, in his Letter to the Galatians, in which "there is no longer Jew or Greek; there is no longer slave or free; there is no longer male and female" (Gal. 3:28).

The first time I taught Women in the Bible in Louisville, Kentucky, one of the women in the group, a seventy-year-old black grandmother, who had raised eight children and was now raising her three grandchildren, sat up at the end of our discussion about Eve, slammed her hand down on the table, and said, "I been listenin' to that Adam's rib shit all my life, and I guess I just don't have to listen to it anymore!" That woman's name was Elcapitola Brown. We called her Cappy. I hope she remembers me.

Tomorrow, at breakfast, I will ask my pioneers what they remember about those Eve lectures. I will ask them what they thought, whether they were shocked. It would take more than a new look at Eve to shock the women I see now on Wednesday mornings; I expect those women of March 2013 might be shocked by the questions they're asking today. I don't know. But I will ask. It always comes back to questions.

⚜

Sometimes we seem to have more information about Eve than about Lydia. Several people have told me that Lydia taught Sunday School at the Granby Street Methodist Episcopal Church, not far from where Captain John Roper would build homes for his children. The church was founded in 1850. John and Lydia arrived in Norfolk in 1865, and Granby Street Methodist Church was waiting for them. Did the Roper family walk to church on Sunday mornings? Did Lydia and John hold the hands of their small children? Did servants carry the babies?

I read the second chapter of Genesis again. Eve listens to God's warning about the Tree of the Knowledge of Good and Evil, and she considers what He has said. She certainly must have heard the threat—"in the day that you eat of it you will die" (Gen. 2:17). She weighs her choices. On the one hand, "the tree was good for food ... a delight to the eyes, and ... was to be desired to make one wise" (Gen. 3:6). On the other hand, the quoted price is death. Is there a different kind of freedom in knowing the price of things?

She considers also what the serpent has said, "You will not die; for ... when you eat of it your eyes will be opened, and you will be like gods, knowing good and evil" (Gen. 3:4-5).

In the Louvre there is a carved libation vase from the twenty-first century BCE, inscribed to "Ningizzida, Lord of the Tree of Life." Ningizzida is sometimes associated with Gilgamesh, the hero of a Sumerian creation myth in which a man is created from the earth, lives in harmony with the animals in an idyllic setting, takes food from a woman, and leaves his innocent life. He is forbidden to return.

Two upwardly spiraling serpents define the vase. In early Mesopotamian culture, the serpent was a god of healing, a symbol of wisdom, and the guardian of treasures and sacred places (*http://www.bibleorigins.net/Serpentningishzida.html* and Joseph Campbell. *The Masks of God: Ancient Mythology*).

Libations to Yahweh are traditional rituals in the Hebrew Scriptures. The Patriarch, Jacob, "took a stone that he had put under his head and set it up for a pillar and poured oil on the top of it" (Gen. 28:18) and, again, after he met God at Bethel, he "set up a pillar in the place where he had spoken with him, a pillar of stone; and he poured out a drink offering on it" (Gen. 35:14). During the Feast of Unleavened Bread, "the drink offering ... shall be of wine" (Leviticus 23:13). But the great Prophet, Isaiah, in a passionate attack on other forms of worship, railed at the unfaithful in Jerusalem, "Among the smooth stones of the valley is your portion; they, they, are your lot; to them you have poured out a drink offering" (Isaiah 57:6). Jacob, setting up altars wherever God led him, was known as the man of stones. The pagan pillars, of course, were fertility symbols, and the exhortation to destroy them became a litany of the Torah and the Prophets.

In the desert, the people complained and "the Lord sent poisonous serpents among the people, and they bit the people, so that many Israelites died" (Numbers 21:6). Then, in what is to become a familiar kind of turnaround, "The Lord said to Moses, 'Make a poisonous serpent, and set it on a pole; and everyone who is bitten shall look at it and live' ... So Moses made a serpent of bronze, and put it on a pole; and ... that person [who had been bitten] would look at the serpent of bronze and live" (21:8-9).

In The Gospel According to John, Jesus says, "And just as Moses lifted up the serpent in the wilderness, so must the Son of Man be lifted up, that whoever believes in him may have eternal life" (John 3:14-15).

In the beginning, at the Lydia Roper Home, bringing stones, and serpents, and libations poured from intricate vases to our study of the Bible, I scattered fragments of ideas, tilled the soil, and waited. It would be a long time before this sowing would come to harvest, a long time before other voices joined mine.

For me, Eve always brings to mind Prometheus, that Greek trickster who broke the rules and stole fire from the gods. The price he paid was unimaginable suffering: he was chained to a rock, where each day his liver would be eaten by an eagle, then grow back to be eaten again the next day. I wonder if even that is more severe than really knowing good and evil. Eve and Adam are cursed by God, not to be chained to a rock, but to suffer pain in childbirth, to dig food out of an unyielding earth, to be separated from each other and from God, to be "lonely forever" (Ted Kooser, "Mother").

In Greek mythology, Prometheus represents the quest for knowledge, which can sometimes end in tragedy. After she dips into that first well of tragedy and knowledge, Eve is named, by Adam, "the mother of all living" (Gen. 3:20).

One of Lydia's great-granddaughters says that Lydia was named for the Lydia of Acts 16:12-15, "a worshipper of God ... and a dealer in purple cloth." The Lydia of Acts does just what the unnamed disciple on the road to Emmaus does: she invites God and his disciples in:

"Stay with us for it is nearly evening," say the disciples to Jesus, "so he went in to stay with them" (Luke 24:13-35); "Come and stay at my house," Lydia implores the apostles, and the writer of Acts tells us, "she prevailed upon us" (Acts 16:15).

We have to ask; we have to invite; we have to insist. At the Lydia Roper Home, as we read the Bible together, we are beginning to insist.

I hope Lydia Roper had just one dress of purple cloth.

I heard a sermon recently about the story of the Patriarch, Jacob, wrestling all night with God. It's a fairly complicated story about a family history of betrayals, in which Jacob is, at the moment when he meets God, on his way home after many years. His mission is reconciliation with his brother, Esau, whom he tricked out of his birthright and their father's deathbed blessing. In the few verses that describe the struggle (Gen. 32:24-32), God, against the odds and after wrestling with Jacob all night, "did not prevail." In a last effort, "when he saw he did not prevail," God strikes Jacob on the hip and knocks it "out of joint." He then demands that Jacob release him, which Jacob refuses to do "unless you bless me." God not only blesses Jacob; he gives him a new name, Israel, and a new identity. Jacob becomes the father of the Twelve Tribes of Israel, the father of the nation, and God tells him, "You have striven with God and with humans, and have prevailed." The name "Israel" means "the one who wrestles with God."

The point of the sermon was that God wants us to hang on and refuse to let go. God challenges us to wrestle with him until we are blessed. Jacob also bestows a name, this time on the place. He calls it "Peniel ... for I have seen God face to face, and yet my life is preserved." And he walks away from Peniel "limping because of his hip." We wrestle; we are blessed; we are wounded.

Jacob Wrestles with the Angel
(Genesis 32:22-32)

Names are sacred; names mean something. Wounds can be a blessing.

Naming is a powerful ritual in the ancient world and in these ancient documents. God names each part of his creation; Adam names the animals and Eve; at each transformative moment in the Hebrew Bible and in the New Testament, naming is involved: Sarai and Abram's names are changed by God to Sarah and Abraham when He promises that "Abraham shall become a great and mighty nation, and all the nations of the earth shall be blessed in him" (Gen. 17:5,15; 18:18); Jacob wrestles with God all night and is renamed Israel (Gen. 32:24-31); the angel who announces the births of the Baptist and the Messiah ordains their names, "Your wife Elizabeth will bear you a son, and you will name him John" (Luke 1:13); "Mary ... you will conceive in your womb and bear a son, and you will name him Jesus" (Luke 1:30-31).

The Jewish *bris*, the ritual of circumcision, and Christian baptism involve the bestowing of a name and the making of a promise. The baptismal ceremony begins significantly with the question, "What name do you give your child?" It ends with the assurance that "you are marked as Christ's own forever" and are received "into the household of God." In the *bris*, the baby is held by an adult who recites the prayer for naming, "Our Lord, and Lord of our ancestors. Establish this child for his father and mother, and may his name be called_____." The word *bris* means covenant, and the father reads, "Blessed are You, God our Lord, King of the Universe, who has ... commanded us to bring this child into the covenant of Abraham." The Christian child is baptized in the name of the Father, the Son, and the Holy Spirit. The Jewish child is welcomed into the line of Abraham, Isaac, and Jacob (http://rabbi4u.com/index.php? option=com_conte nt&task=view&id=19&Itemid=75).

The Roper family trails names like banners behind them: John and Lydia, Margaret, Virginia, Isabel, Albert, Leighton, Molly and George. Like Eve and Sarah, Adam and Abraham, like Jacob, who is Israel, these names mean something. The names of the ladies at the Roper Home mean something, too.

⚜

One morning, I arrived almost an hour before breakfast and climbed up to Nan's third floor corner room, a large space with extra windows, including a dormer. It's an atticky kind of place, with more personality than rooms down the hall or on lower floors. I find Nan still in her purple silk nightgown, brushing her teeth. We talk while she dresses, two women comfortable in each other's company. Finally, I ask her about her name; it's Nanette Lucille. Her mother was Lucille, her grandmother Bertha. She can't remember further back than that, and she doesn't know where they found "Nanette." She thinks that "Nan" suits her just right. When I ask why her answer is "because I'm short." A good morning laugh, and I ask how she's feeling. I know she almost always wakes up in pain. "Very bad; when I woke up I felt so discouraged. Then you came in." I was worrying that I was intruding, and here it is. What we are doing here matters.

＊ＳＯＢＣＳＡ

As I recall my study of Eve with the ladies at Lydia Roper, I work hard to locate in time and place the women of the Roper clan, into which Lydia Hand Bowen married in the summer of 1865: women born to Lydia; and women marrying Roper men—initiates, carrying their new names like baptized children. They are Margaret and Virginia, Lydia's only daughters; George's first wife, Isabelle Place Hayward, and his second, Maida Secor, an artist whose painting hangs in the Lydia Roper Home; Georgiane, who married Albert Roper, and gave birth to a son, Leighton, and to another Margaret, Caroline's mother; Ethel May, Albert's second and younger wife; Molly Jernigan Winborne Roper, Leighton's wife and mother of Leighton and Albert and of Molly Jernigan Roper Jenkins, who lives now near the Blue Ridge Mountains, two hundred miles from the port city where her great-grandfather founded his Virginia empire and built his Norfolk houses; and Caroline, cousin of Molly and Leighton and Albert, whose life is on the other coast, three thousand miles away from both fiefdom and family.

It is Wednesday morning in Norfolk, June 18, 2014. I am up especially early to catch my ride at seven so I can make it to the Roper Home in time for breakfast and the visit I have planned with the ladies. I want to know about their first impressions of the Bible Study, but I don't want to take our Bible Study time to do that. This way, I can sit with them in the dining room, laptop on the table, and type while I listen. The last time I came for breakfast they told me they were getting used to this new way of communicating with me. I think I believe them; they're still telling stories. And it is, we are coming to see, all about stories: Bible stories, Roper stories, the stories of this house, our stories. It's the stories we tell in the dark to make some sense of it all.

Ready to go ahead of time, I have a few minutes to think about the way the Lydia Roper Home appeared to me a year ago. From where I sat at my old table, I faced a large and imposing piece of furniture, a kind of sideboard with a nearly black finish, carved elaborately with flowers, vaguely disturbing faces, and oddly assorted human figures. One day last month I went in early just to examine that piece more closely. It really is remarkable. Some

of the faces are only half human, encircled by hair like lions'
manes; they look like Egyptian sun kings. The figures are of men
in crowns and royal robes and of pregnant women, naked, arms
folded protectively over their bellies. I searched the Internet for
something similar and found a nineteenth century hunting board
breakfront, carved with tall figures of nearly naked men and
women, the men with lions' manes and regal cloaks, the women
pregnant. These carvings are primitive. More searching turned
up several more, all dating from between 1860 and 1930, most
mahogany. Al thinks that maybe Lydia and John's son George
built the piece. A local historian says it was in the Jamestown
Exhibition of 1907. In any case, there it sits, dominating the room.
I have recently heard there are plans to get rid of the breakfront;
it's hard to imagine why. Two staff members have told me it's one
of the things people notice when they tour.

As it turns out, my ride comes early and I get to the Lydia
Roper Home by seven-thirty. Lucille and Cora Mae are already
downstairs, sitting in the chairs that are lined up against the
walls outside the dining room. This is where we all come to wait
before meals. The doors to the dining room are paned glass,
opening into the room, and they stay closed with a chain across
them until the kitchen crew is ready for us. There is usually a
group gathered out here far enough ahead of mealtime for some
good talk. This half hour or more before meals is one of the
times during the day when everyone seems relaxed and ready to
unbutton a little. And here comes Neal. I ask her, and have just
asked Lucille, what they thought about the Bible Study when
they first got there.

From Lucille, "It was good; I just felt like there were things
God wants me to know and you were talking about some of them."

Sometimes I forget that they don't remember. They don't
know what we were reading, have forgotten what it seemed like,
don't know why they kept coming.

Neal, "The stroke ruined me; I used to remember everything.
I can't remember what I felt like the first time I came; I just
know I kept coming back." Neal is eighty-one and she thinks she
had her stroke more than a year ago.

There is no experience quite like walking through that front
door; the emptiness is complete and intimate. You feel it as a

weight on your chest; breathing is difficult. The bits of your life that you are able to carry—the photographs, the few pieces of furniture, some pictures for the walls—only make it clearer that you have lost, not only any hope of a future, but your past. I remember wishing my children hadn't come ahead of me and set up my room to look like home; it mocked me every day. You are displaced in time, among strangers, nowhere. Together, in this unlikely place, these "Bible ladies" and I have forged an anchor for ourselves. On Wednesday mornings we are secured; we belong; we are still alive; we are somewhere.

Evelyn is here now, maneuvering her walker around so she can sit across from me. Her earrings are gold loops, dolphins curled in on each other, a gift from her daughter. She does recall the first Bible Study and thinks maybe Wilma was there, too. Evelyn, Inez, Kate, possibly Wilma. Now I seem to remember that Mrs. Grantly came. I know she was there sometime while we were still in the downstairs living room; I can see her, sound asleep in her chair, paperback mystery clutched tightly in one hand. I need more help, someone else's memory. I do remember little Melanie, who never missed a session, made faces at me from across the room, and periodically shouted out, "Oh, shut up." During the month between my move and my return to start the New Testament, Melanie left the Lydia Roper Home.

At the end of one of his least known poems, "Bereft," Robert Frost wrote, "Word I was in the house alone/Somehow must have gotten abroad/Word I was in my life alone/Word I had no one left but God."

Someone sounds the chime; the doors open, and in we go. Nan arrives in a pair of white slacks and a blue and tan print shirt, sleeves rolled to the elbow, a vivid blue shell underneath. Gena used to share that table. She, too, is gone. I'm suddenly aware of the empty chairs, the women I saw every day who are no longer here: Nan's Gena; Cindy, leaving a chair still unoccupied next to Kate and Inez; Louise with her quiet refrain of "Where am I supposed to be?"; Mrs. Grantly; little Melanie; and Gerty who always brought her own tea and jam to breakfast. Alice, my suite mate for several months, died last year.

I am at the table now with Kate and Inez. These two women were there at the very first Bible Study and they have stuck it out for well over a year. I'd like to know why. We are pretty hopeless this morning, none of us remembering much about the beginning of this thing, nor when it started to change.

Inez does recall that she liked it right away because "it reminded me of everything I had learned in Sunday School."

I grew up in the Episcopal church and didn't get that kind of familiarity with the Bible. I sometimes went to Sunday School with my Baptist friends just to hear the Bible stories, but I didn't really start reading the Bible until that course in graduate school.

Kate remembers we didn't have handouts, although she mentions an outline for Cain and Abel. I realize that we wouldn't have talked much about Cain and Abel until the second time through the Old Testament, when we focused on stories about the men, so that doesn't take us closer to the beginning. I'm wondering, all of a sudden, if this might go better when we're all together, helping each other remember with our bits and pieces of memory. In spite of not wanting to spare the time, maybe I'll try it in a couple of weeks, once we've made a good start on Acts.

But Acts is now, in June of 2014, and we are struggling with what calls to us from the last cold months of 2013. Eve and Adam; Adam and Eve: Names to conjure with, names we all know, names we learned from the cradle, no matter what our upbringing. Even if we were raised with no religion, even if we never read the Bible or even heard the stories, we heard those names. I can never forget Cappy Brown's moment of revelation, "I guess I just don't have to listen to it anymore!" Some of the younger women who read the stories with me in Kentucky said that once they talked at home about what we were doing, their husbands and boyfriends started bringing them flowers. The power of stories is evident right from the first verse of the first chapter of the book of Genesis: "In the beginning God created the heaven and the earth. And the earth was without form and void, and darkness was upon the face of the deep. And the Spirit of God moved upon the face of the waters" (Gen. 1:1-2). Can there be a bigger story than that?

I wonder today about the stories I put on the table back there at the beginning—the charged questions I asked, the edgy ideas about our Judaeo-Christian tradition. Was it too much? I invited these women, to whom I was a complete stranger, to entertain some radical possibilities. But so we began, wisely or not, and so we have continued. On the first day, there was Eve, the weak link, the temptress, the sinner who is responsible for all the pain and suffering in the world, who seduced Adam into sin. I read aloud what the story actually says. "She gave some to her husband, *who was with her* [my italics], and he ate." He was "with her" all along; he, too, heard the serpent. I have always had difficulty finding a seduction here. I remember that I talked to these women about my own perception of Eve as a hero who stole knowledge from the gods.

I know I must have questioned the age-old stereotype that women have pain in childbirth because we are sinful, and the idea that Eve's punishment was worse than Adam's (proving, of course, that her sin was worse) because all he had to do was farm. I almost certainly said I didn't think so.

"I will greatly increase your pangs in childbearing; in pain you shall bring forth children, yet your desire shall be for your husband, and he shall rule over you" (Gen. 3:16).

Admittedly not nothing, a harsh sentence for just eating some forbidden fruit. Of course, the fruit isn't really the point, is it? It's the disobedience. Who does this woman think she is? So, lots of children, painfully got, and the desire that will keep her getting more, a detail that's often omitted from Sunday sermons. When you think about it, a lusty sexuality is an odd punishment. An ironic, as well as a jealous, God.

"And to the man he said, 'Cursed is the ground because of you; in toil you shall eat of it all the days of your life; thorns and thistles it shall bring forth for you; and you shall eat the plants of the field. By the sweat of your face you shall eat bread until you return to the ground, for out of it you were taken; you are dust and to dust you shall return" (Gen. 3:17-19).

Now here is an impressive consequence of bad behavior: because of Adam, the entire earth is cursed.

And the very next thing that happens is that Adam names Eve, "the mother of all living" (Gen. 3:20).

An intriguing response to all this pain and suffering he's about to encounter.

And they are "sent forth from the garden of Eden," Adam to "till the ground from which he was taken."

The question I remember asking, which at that point in our Bible Study I had to answer for myself, was "What exactly has happened here? Is this simply a story of sin and punishment? "

I know how I answer; I know how I have answered for thirty years. I can't remember how I answered a year ago as I talked with the ladies at the Lydia Roper Home. I recall with an almost physical clarity that living room on the first floor with its tall windows that let in the thin winter light, making the space seem even larger and emptier than it was. I see the four or five of us, sitting in chairs placed in a wide circle, keeping us as far away from each other as possible, and I am grateful for our small crowded parlor upstairs.

This journey is partly about the spaces we inhabit. I started months ago to write the story of the Bible Study and the women at the Lydia Roper Home. Fairly soon, I realized that I needed a short history of the building to provide background. I discovered no one was quite sure about the details, and the written records were hard to pin down and often contradictory. I was encountering obstacles where I hadn't expected them. Finally, just recently, the construction of the house was confirmed, commissioned by Captain Roper in 1920, designed by the Norfolk architectural firm of Peebles and Ferguson. By that time, the pursuit of the basic facts was getting easier, and I even found, almost by mistake, that Mr. Peebles was on the team of architects that designed the impressive Epworth Methodist Church in its present home on Freemason Street.

The story began when Captain Jack Roper returned to Norfolk, Virginia, in 1865, the year the Civil War ended, carrying with him the money from his California gold mine. According to family lore, when he returned from California in 1861, he had a thousand dollars. He immediately signed up as a soldier in the Union Army. Concerned that he might die in the war, he left that money with a friend for his mother's care. The friend invested it and when John got home and reclaimed his money, it had grown to ten thousand dollars. With that stake, he built a state-of-the-art saw mill in Princess Anne County, Virginia, and started cutting timber and shipping lumber for men in other cities to plan the rooms and build the houses that would hold their women and children.

With very little effort I found out about Captain Roper and the Roper Land and Lumber Company. He was what the historians call a carpetbagger, but by the end of the century he was erecting his own houses, mostly of brick, large, imposing, solid houses for his family and for his sons and daughters and their families. Eventually, John and Lydia lived in the main house; George, in a house on the same block; Margaret and Ginny in two houses side by side. Around the corner, two more sons had their homes. Captain Jack Roper kept a tight rein on his family.

Norfolk's population after the war was around nineteen thousand. The Norfolk shipyard, burned by evacuating Federal troops in 1861 and burned again by the retreating Confederate army in 1862, was in ruins, but the rest of the city was largely intact, having been occupied by the Union army during the last years of the war. Northern businessmen had been moving into Norfolk for at least two years, so Captain Roper wasn't unusual or unexpected. His swift and near complete mastery of the lumber industry in Virginia and North Carolina, however, was both.

A story: In 1887, the John L. Roper Land and Lumber Company set up shop in Lee's Mill, North Carolina, and on August 14, 1889, the name of Lee's Mill was changed to Roper. In 1906 the town of Roper was chartered, and it "became a boomtown. During its peak, the Roper Lumber Company was the biggest supplier of cedar shingles in the United States (http://en.wikipedia.org/wiki/Norfolk_Southern_Railway(1942–82), and before 1900 its landed interests consisted of more than two hundred thousand acres. Roper, North Carolina, is still there, population six hundred eleven at the 2010 census. The median income for a household in the town is just over twenty thousand dollars (http://en.wikipedia.org/wiki/Roper,_North_Carolina).

Another story: In North Carolina, there was a town called Wonderland, a logging camp owned by the Roper Lumber Company. Some claim that the name Wonderland came from the peat fires that burned beneath the surface in the Great Dismal Swamp, then exploded, sometimes burning "houses, livestock and, they said, at least 1 child." The Smithsonian National Postal Museum lists a post office at Wonderland from June 1918 until October 1925. Someone born in 1937, in a community adjoining Wonderland, writes that at that time, "the area called Wonderland, was still called Wonderland, but there was nothing left of the camps. The railroad was gone, taken up completely" (http://blogs.lib.unc.edu/ncm/index.php/2008/07/18/lost-wonderland/).

Between 1865 and the turn of the century, Norfolk was struggling with Reconstruction and only made a kind of peace with the results of the war in 1869 when Virginia voted to ratify the Fourteenth and Fifteenth Amendments. John Roper's particular peace was eased by his commitment to philanthropy in his adopted city. He was President of United Charities, which he helped found, and was involved with the Union Mission. He helped organize the Masonic Relief Association, through which the Masonic Temple was built. In 1893, Captain Roper helped finance a home for unwed mothers, establishing shelters for women all over the city. He was instrumental in starting the Women's College of Norfolk. In 1921 construction was completed on the Colonial Revival building on East 40th Street, and the Lydia Roper Home received its charter.

John Roper's father died when John was an infant and his mother, Esther Ann Reynolds Roper, raised him on her own. There were two other children, a boy and a girl. The girl stayed at home; as soon as she could, Esther apprenticed the boys out. She got some work as a seamstress, but she couldn't afford to feed three children. John adored her. In his handwritten autobiography, barely legible in places, he mentions her on nearly every page. Settled in Norfolk, he set about providing for women.

In that same autobiography, John Roper mentions his wife, Lydia, once: "I returned to Philadelphia and married my wife Miss Lydia H. Bowen, daughter of David H. Bowen. Our wedding trip consisted of our return to Norfolk for several weeks."

⁂

I have learned a great deal about the Roper family but almost nothing about Lydia. Not a word beyond the public records: date of birth; place of birth; date of marriage; dates of children's births; death; burial. Nothing. Where is she? Where are her belongings? Did she receive letters from her family in Philadelphia? From friends? Did she save small items—a handkerchief, a glove, a cameo, one earring? I think about Evelyn's earrings: where will they go when she dies? Lydia's great-grandchildren tell me about trunks of family keepsakes. Where are Lydia's keepsakes? She was the matriarch of a large and prominent family, a family with a strong sense of "family." Even given the times, she is too well hidden. I will spend a day at the library searching in Philadelphia records; she was there for twenty-five years before she married and moved south. What was she doing? Why hadn't she married earlier? What was her life? At twenty-five she must have had one.

And I know now what my questions for Lydia will be, should I find her: What did you want? What did you get? What did you lose? We don't know when Lydia met John Roper, but she saw something in this veteran of the California gold mines and the battlefields of Virginia, headed south with dreams of fortune, that allowed her to walk away from that Philadelphia life and go with him. What was Lydia Hand Bowen after? What dream was she chasing?

These are the questions I want to ask the ladies at the Lydia Roper Home. These are the questions I will ask myself as we gather to talk: What did we want? What did we get? What did we lose?

What dreams were we chasing?

⚜

For the moment, I step back from these stories of Captain John Roper and Lydia Bowen Roper, from these Norfolk stories, these Virginia stories, these southern stories, and return to the morning dining room to think about the stories the ladies at the Roper Home will tell; those are the stories I long to hear. They have told me parts of those stories across time, in scraps and pieces, sometimes whispered in hallways or in rare moments alone in the downstairs living room or in our refuge on the second floor when we have wandered in early. Now I want to know more than pieces and scraps. Yesterday at breakfast we discussed whether they'd rather talk about themselves just to me, or in the group. They all agreed it would be more fun to talk together.

The tale of the Garden of Eden is not a story about sin and punishment; it's a story of how we grow up.

While we wait for our own storytelling, there are the Roper women, all around.

There is, first of all, John L. Roper's mother, born in 1811 in Mifflin County, Pennsylvania. We don't know when Esther moved to Norfolk to be with her son and Lydia, but she died here in 1885 and is interred in the family mausoleum.

Margaret, John and Lydia's oldest daughter, was born in 1866 in Philadelphia, eight years before her sister, Virginia, Lydia's only other daughter. These were the Roper women of the second generation, occupants of the double-house.

When Lydia's daughter Margaret was barely twenty she was already involved with a group of young, well-to-do women from Granby Street Methodist Church who wanted to help the poor in Norfolk. They knew about the International Order of The King's Daughters and Sons, part of whose guiding principle was "lend a hand," and, in 1886, Margaret was among those who formed the first King's Daughters Circle in Norfolk. By 1896, Margaret was taking the lead, and an online history of the King's Daughters gives her full credit, "With the vision of a King's Daughter named Miss Margaret Roper, the Circles came together ... forming the Norfolk City Union of the King's Daughters." Caroline, Lydia's great-granddaughter, remembers her "Tante Margaret" taking her to an old brick building in which there was a facility for mothers and their babies. In 1913, The King's Daughters established a Baby Clinic, the first step toward what would become the King's Daughters Children's Hospital (https://www.kingsdaughters.org/who-we-are/history/).

We don't know when Ginny and well-known Richmond artist Adele Williams became friends, but in 1907, Ginny, age thirty-three, was a bridesmaid at the wedding of Adele's brother, Victor Williams, in Richmond. A retrospective of Adele's art in the

Summer 1992 issue of the *Virginia Cavalcade* describes Ginny as "a shy but very talented amateur musician and composer," who "posed for her portrait in the weeks just after the ceremony." Family members confirm that "for many years [Ginny's] family provided Adele Williams with a studio on the grounds of their summer estate at Blue Ridge Summit, Pennsylvania, where, according to Molly Roper, wife of Ginny's nephew, 'all the flowers they grew were grown for Adele to paint.'"

I have seen a portrait of a young woman who might or might not be Virginia Roper, by an artist who might or might not be Adele Williams. The woman in the portrait can't be much older than twenty. She is very beautiful.

No story accompanies this painting; there are no exciting details beyond the canvas. It is not signed. The painting stands on its own.

In 1915, Margaret married George Farant Moss, a cotton broker from Flat Creek, North Carolina. George was 52; Margaret was 49. Neither had been married before.

Ginny Roper never married.

On January 22, 1913, in a small ceremony in the chapel of St. Bartholomew's Episcopal Church in Manhattan, Georgiane Phillips Parks, daughter of Leighton Parks, well-known radical minister and rector of St. Bartholomew's, married Albert Lonsdale Roper, attorney and future three-term mayor of Norfolk, Virginia. The Bishop performed the ceremony in the church's small chapel. According to *The New York Times* of January 23 of that year, "It was a quiet affair, few invitations being issued. Miss Parks had no attendants."

Family legends include the story of Georgiane's buggy-whipping a man in downtown Norfolk because he was beating his horse.

On November 6, 1901, in New York City, George Wisham Roper, Lydia and John's first born son and the first chairman of the Lydia Roper Home's Board of Trustees, married Isabelle Place Hayward.

In May of 1915, at the age of forty-one, Isabelle died; she is interred in her husband's mausoleum at Cedar Grove Cemetery.

"Sometime after 1915 and before 1930," (one source says definitely 1930) George married a second time: Matilda Secor McCord, known as Maida, was forty-four. Ancestry records list under "occupation" for Matilda McCord: "artist; exhibited in France, Italy and America."

A watercolor of the Roper breakfront, signed Maida Secor Roper, hangs in the dining room of the Roper Home, on the wall across from the breakfront itself. The colors of the painting suggest a much paler, and less formidable, piece of furniture. In the foreground of the painting is a formal dining table, a small brass bowl of flowers in the center, a dark Victorian armchair at either end. Underneath is an oriental rug, just large enough to accommodate table and chairs. In the background is the open door to the kitchen.

Of the women who married into the Roper family, Maida Secor was an artist; Georgiane Phillips Parks wrote under the assumed name of George Phillips. Lydia's daughter, Ginny, was a musician and composer, and her close friend, Adele Williams, was renowned worldwide as a painter in the Impressionist style. Her watercolors hang in museums and in private collections; they are rare and expensive.

On March 12, 1930, Georgiane Roper died, at the age of forty-eight, and was buried on her husband's lot in Elmwood Cemetery in Norfolk. Her death certificate reads, "Postpartum Complications." Georgiane's only daughter was eleven.

On Tuesday, December 9, 1930, Lydia Hand Roper was interred in the John Lonsdale Roper Mausoleum in Elmwood Cemetery. Funeral services were held at the residence at 314 Freemason Street in Norfolk. The Norfolk newspaper, *The Ledger*, reports that "there was a very large attendance" at the Roper home but "interment was private."

It is Thursday morning July 3, 2014. I am looking over the papers I printed at the library on Tuesday, getting ready for a return trip today. In the 1910 Federal Census for Margaret Bowen Roper, under the heading, "Mother," I read "Liddy H. Roper." Lydia Roper, the Lydia Hand Bowen Roper of my now daily search, at one moment of her life, might have been called, by someone, Liddy. Was it a nickname her parents gave her? Did her husband call her "Liddy"? Was it a name Lydia liked for herself? Who answered the door that day when the census taker knocked, looking for Margaret Bowen Roper, age forty-four? Was it Margaret? Was it Lydia, now seventy? Did the census taker simply misunderstand the name? I choose to believe he did not. As I walk to the market with a palpable sense of her, I make a decision to believe that Liddy Roper existed, even if I never find her. Names mean something.

Eve was named "the mother of all living," which, in other translations, reads, "the lady of the rib." The story of the Garden is about the growing up and the living we all have to do. It is about that of which we are a part.

In a final attempt to recall a few more specifics from that morning over a year ago when four or five women and I sat down to study the Bible, I go back through my computer files from decades of Bible classes.

I find myself back in the Garden and I wonder if I talked last year about the *felix culpa*, a Latin phrase that translates: *the happy or fortunate fall*. I think I must have, if only because it's an idea that has always fascinated me. It seems to get the whole crew from Eden right off the hook. The theory is that the sin, the disobedience, in that primal setting, was really the best thing that could have happened. God knew what He was up to all along; Eve and Adam acted exactly as intended. St. Augustine, born in the year 354, wrote that "God judged it better to bring good out of evil than not to permit any evil to exist." And a later sage of the Church, Thomas Aquinas, writing in the thirteenth century, added, "God allows evils to happen in order to bring a greater good therefrom." The phrase is central to the Easter Vigil mass of the Catholic Church, "Oh happy fault that earned for us so great, so glorious a Redeemer." In other words, without Eve's disobedience, we wouldn't have Jesus. Why isn't she a hero, or at least redeemed? Without evil, there could be no good. Adam and Eve seem, by this reckoning, to have been nothing worse than pawns. The serpent, reduced to a huckster with a few tricks up his sleeve, plays his role convincingly and ends up crawling on his belly.

And do we now have an answer to that old question of Western religion: If God is all good, and all powerful, why is there evil in the world? Not quite. We haven't asked the sufferers of all that necessary evil what they think. And no matter how you read it, down through the millennia, Eve is left holding the bag.

❧❦❧

Just this week, we talked about what "in the name of Jesus" means; Catherine always prays for someone's healing "in the name of Jesus." I asked this question: If I am very sick, and my neighbors, who are not Christians, stay up all night praying for me, but definitely not in the name of Jesus, will God hear those prayers? Will they be effective? Names are important; with a name I can conjure God.

When Eve isn't the cause of sin, and suffering, and death, she is something else entirely. In Genesis 2:22, most English translations say that God provided a "helpmeet" or "helpmate" for Adam. It's an odd translation. Among the early understandings of the Hebrew word *ezer* are "power," "strength," and "savior." In the Hebrew Bible, the word appears twenty times. In seventeen of those, it refers to God. The second word of the phrase is *k'enegdo*, best understood as a mirror opposite; the image is of two people facing each other. God created for Adam a saving power or strength corresponding to himself (Gen. 2:18) (http://www.womeninthescriptures.com/2010/11/real-meaning-of-term-help-meet.html) and (http://www.cbeinternational.org/blogs/does-it-really-mean-helpmate).

Names mean something; words matter.

"In the beginning, God created the heaven and the earth. And the earth was without form, and void, and darkness was upon the face of the deep. And the Spirit of God moved upon the face of the waters" (Gen. 1:1-2).

⁂

The darkness was already lifting in Norfolk in the year 1865. The Port of Norfolk was busy; the town was full of immigrating Northerners here for easy money. Reconstruction was under way, and a new life was beginning for the Commonwealth. Captain Jack Roper intended to be part of that beginning. His wife, Lydia, came with him. We know so little of her, a hundred and fifty years later. Jack Roper arrived in Norfolk and became a visible presence. Did Lydia Hand Bowen Roper arrive in Norfolk and disappear? For three generations, her great-grandson, Albert, tells me that "nobody ever talked about her."

I discover that John Roper did not begin his great adventure in Virginia alone, as almost all the information about him suggests. One entry about John Roper in *The History of Norfolk County*, describes the start of the company: in 1865, "in partnership with Francis R. Baird ... [Roper] established the lumber business ... of which he is now the head." In fact, for nearly a dozen years, the John L. Roper Lumber Company didn't exist; the company to which John Roper belonged was known as Baird & Roper. Only at Francis Baird's death in 1876 did it assume the name it was to carry into the twentieth century and with which it would carry John L. Roper to fame and fortune in the Virginia and North Carolina lumber industries (http://www.mocavo.com/ History-of-Norfolk-County-Virginia-and-Representative-Citize ns-1637-1900/444848/561).

I have found no stories about Francis R. Baird. The only trace of him is his Last Will and Testament, entered in March of 1877 in the city of Norfolk. If you enter Mr. Baird's name into an Internet search engine, the will is the only "hit."

⁂

The Bible ladies who reside at the Lydia Roper Home today refuse to be invisible. They sit in their comfortable chairs, questioning the most basic assumptions, wrestling with God, one floor above the portraits of Lydia and John Roper. No one has yet told me Lydia's story, but the stories of all of us gathered here will be told in defiance of that.

Chapter Four

THE STORIES WE TELL

"WE TELL OURSELVES STORIES in order to live"
(Joan Didion, *The White Album*).

"A need to tell and hear stories is essential to the species
Homo Sapiens—second in necessity apparently after
nourishment and before love and shelter. Millions survive
without love or home, almost none in silence ... and the sound
of story is the dominant sound of our lives"
(Reynolds Price, *A Palpable God*).

A Palpable God is a collection of Price's own translations of thirty stories from the Bible. They are the great stories, known and not so familiar: the stories of Joseph and Potiphar's wife; of the binding of Isaac and of the rape of Dinah; of the resurrection of Jesus; of David's unseemly dancing of the Ark into Jerusalem; and of the New Jerusalem promised at the apocalypse. Every story rings with "the dominant sound of our lives." And every story demands to be told.

I have found some wonderful stories, but I have not found

Lydia Roper's story. I am not ready to give up. I am not ready to give up because I have fallen in love with this woman whose story I have failed to find. I am not ready to give up because this has become a search for stories. At the Lydia Roper Home, we are reading stories and telling stories and listening to stories. We are coming to understand that stories, like names, are important, and our list of stories is getting longer. It does not include Lydia's story.

I am not ready to give up looking for Lydia because I want to know what Lydia was looking for. What did she want? What dream was she chasing? What did she get?

Toward the end of a cold Winter, the ladies at the Roper Home and I were looking for a better understanding of the Bible, or for companionship, or just for a way to spend a couple of hours a week. I was looking to survive; maybe we all were. Now we are also looking for Lydia.

I am not ready to give up.

⚜

Every week I do what I've done since March of 2013: I read the Scriptures; I read commentary; I type handouts; I think. On Wednesday mornings since November, I travel to the Lydia Roper Home and talk about the Bible and listen to the kind of talk about the Bible that none of us could have imagined. Last Spring, when we had completed our reading of the first three chapters of Genesis, I decided to simply keep going in the Hebrew Scriptures, staying focused on the women in some of the most important stories. I know those stories well. So much of our reading of both Hebrew and New Testament narratives is about the men: Abraham, Isaac, and Jacob; Moses; Saul; David; Solomon; Joshua at the battle of Jericho; Jesus himself, Peter and Paul—the patriarchs, prophets, warriors, the messiah and his disciples. I have a friend, an Episcopal priest, who always says in his celebration of the Eucharist, "The God of Abraham, Isaac, and Jacob; the God of Sarah, Rebekah, and Rachel" (BCP, Eucharistic Prayer C, HE II, 372). Often, instead of these wives of the patriarchs, he calls out the names of women with more difficult credentials: the God of Hagar; the God of Delilah; the God of Jael. It is a solution of sorts.

One of the reasons I have always loved the Hebrew Bible is that its female characters are irresistibly complicated. There are very few who fit the stereotypes of whore and virgin perpetrated by Christianity at its worst. The story I was told said that Eve and Mary were responsible for delivering into the world first sin, then redemption from that sin. But the story of Eve is not a story about sin, and Eve is not a sexual profligate who seduces her husband into sin by making a pact with the devil. We have to read the text. She and Adam are expelled from the Garden of Eden, not because they sinned, but because they might "take also from the tree of life, and eat, and live forever" (Gen. 3:22). The word, 'sin', does not even appear in the Bible until the story of Cain and Abel. The idea of original sin is a fourth century Christian construct fueled by the writings of St. Augustine. The story of the Garden nowhere mentions sex, nowhere describes Adam's eating of the forbidden fruit as a seduction, and nowhere identifies the serpent with Satan. An online essay on original sin (whatjewsbelieve.org) points out the logical fallacy: if Adam and Eve had to eat of the Tree of Life to become immortal, they must have been created mortal to begin with. Death was always part of the deal. The result of this tendency to read "into" the story, rather than actually reading the story, is that we lose the evocative character of Eve in the indelible image of the seductive sinner.

By the time we had reached the story of another of the Hebrew Bible's women, Rebekah, wife of Isaac, mother of Jacob and Esau, we had the second of the large-print handouts, still fairly basic in content. In Rebekah's outline, I had added to the plot summary a few entries under the heading of "Themes." I called attention to the active and decisive young woman who makes up her mind, against her parents' wishes, to leave home without delay on a journey to marry a stranger, the young woman who, against the dictates of convention, "when she saw Isaac ... slipped quickly from the camel" (Gen. 24:64). It is a large part of our first impression of Rebekah (evident even in translation) that the description of her is packed with verbs. From her first appearance at the well where she encountered Abraham's servant, Rebekah was "coming out with her water jar" and "went down to the spring, filled her jar, and came up ... quickly lowered her jar upon her hand and gave

Rebekah at the Well
(Genesis 24: 45-49)

Rebekah meets Isaac by the Way
Genesis 24: 62-65)

him to drink ... quickly emptied her jar and ran again to the well to draw, and ... drew for all the camels ... Then ... ran and told her mother's household about these things" (24: 15, 16, 18, 20, 28). The story vibrates with her energy. There is no mistaking who is in control of the scene.

And the woman who will marry the patriarch, conceive, then challenge God directly about her difficult pregnancy, "If it is to be this way, why do I live?" (25:22), is filled with confidence. She also has a great sense of drama, which serves her well in the scheme she devises to secure a birthright and blessing for her favorite son. The suspense mounts when Rebekah listens outside her husband's door (27:5), then not only convinces Jacob to deceive his father but cooks the stew and lays on the furs that will disguise him (27:14-17). From the beginning, the self-assured Rebekah offers no reasons for her preferences, no excuses for her plotting, and the narrator tells us that "Isaac loved Esau, because he was fond of game; but Rebekah loved Jacob" (25:28). When our urge to see Rebekah as a manipulative and dishonorable woman is strongest, probably when we see the pathetic, nearly blind Isaac, or hear the plaintive cry of despair from Esau when he knows what has happened, we are never allowed to forget that it was God himself who instructed her, at the moment of her loud complaint, that "two nations are in your womb ... the one shall be stronger than the other, the elder shall serve the younger" (25:23). Jacob emerges last, "his hand gripping Esau's heel" (25:26). And whether we view her as a betrayer of her husband's trust and a corrupter of her son's morals, or as the instrument of God's will, I don't think there is anywhere in Scripture a more poignant study of motherhood than this simple statement, "but Rebekah loved Jacob."

Although we have now spent five months on the New Testament and have discussed women, most recently in Luke's Gospel, where there is a large female cast, I find myself often dissatisfied with suffering Mary, the mother of Jesus, with saintly Martha, even with the forgiven sinner with the alabaster jar. I can't think of a single saint in the Hebrew Scriptures. There are wonderful examples of just plain goodness: Ruth and Naomi come immediately to mind, as does Rahab who saves the day for Joshua, then turns up in the New Testament as an ancestor of Jesus (Matt. 1:5), as a woman of faith (Hebrews 11:31) and of good works (James 2:25). But Naomi's very name means "bitterness," and Ruth seduces Boaz on the threshing floor; Rahab is a prostitute. Good, absolutely, but neither saintly nor suffering.

What am I looking for in this text? I have said that my reading of the Gospels this time has been different, transformed by the experience of both studying them and, much more important, of spending week after week thinking about them out loud with the women of the Lydia Roper Home. The reading is new for me because I have been willing to look underneath my own bias, which has told me that the characters in the Hebrew Bible are just more interesting. Perhaps it is the fact that the veneer over the Hebrew Scriptures is thinner; raw human nature, in the shedding of blood, in the laying of plots, in the dishonorable behavior that often serves God's purposes, sometimes in an anthropomorphic God himself, lies close to the surface.

In the New Testament narrative, I have to look harder, dig with more determination below the surface of a text that is written by believers for believers. I have to search for Mary's horrifying vulnerability and courage; Martha's desperate eagerness to please the rabbi from Nazareth; Magdalene's struggle with her demons. Is she so different from Jacob wrestling all night with a "man" (Gen. 32:24)? The Gospels were written over a period of less than a century; the Hebrew Scriptures span well over five centuries. A great deal of complexity can slip into a text in five hundred years.

In fact, the Gospel According to Luke is filled with compelling women: women who follow Jesus from his birth to the cross; women who support the ministry "out of their resources" (Luke 8:3); women who are healed or transformed by Jesus; prominent women; women who wait; women who, in fact, meet all the requirements for discipleship (Mary Ann Getty-Sullivan. *Women In the New Testament*). The full passage from Luke spotlights a tantalizing and suggestive moment in the ministry of Jesus, on the road with his followers: "Soon afterwards [Jesus] went on through cities and villages, proclaiming and bringing the good news of the kingdom of God. The Twelve were with him, as well as some women who had been cured of evil spirits and infirmities. Mary, called Magdalene, from whom seven demons had gone out, and Joanna, the wife of Herod's steward Chuza, and Suzanna, and many others, who provided for them out of their resources" (Luke 8:1-3). In all the Synoptic Gospels, but especially in Luke, the contrast between the women and the disciples provides frequent comic relief. Over and over, the men try hard—you can almost see them furrowing their brows with the effort—but just fail to "get it", while the women quickly and instinctively understand. At the cross, the men flee; the women remain, silent witnesses. It is the women who prepare oil and spices to anoint Jesus' body and, at the tomb on the day of Jesus' resurrection, it is Mary Magdalene who finally recognizes and believes, "I have seen the Lord!" (John 20:18).

I have a bad moment as I realize that in our reading of the Synoptic Gospels we never actually talked about Mary Magdalene. How can I have forgotten her? She is the second most important woman in the Gospels, only after Mary, the mother of Jesus. I pull out the calendar that maps our New Testament study all the way through May of 2015. I confront my own habitual sense of urgency. I'm always in a rush; in my mind, I'm pushing a deadline. My first thought is that we can't possibly make time to spend two weeks on Mary Magdalene or anyone else. We have a schedule. In fact—of course— we have all the time we need; does anyone really care whether we read Revelation in May or in July of 2015? I can sense the absurdity of even the rhetorical question. And besides, Catherine has already explained that it's going to take us three times as long as I've planned to read Revelation. I spend an hour rewriting the calendar.

We will use Ignatian Reflections and *lectio divina* with Magdalene; we will read the short passages three times each; we will pay attention; we will slow down.

In an essay on meditation, a Jesuit priest writes that the goal of Ignatian spirituality is "to discern the footprints of God in our own experience" (Fleming 2008).

Father Dennis Hamm, SJ, Scripture Professor at Creighton University, describes the Ignatian ritual of daily prayer, called the Examen, as "rummaging for God" (http://www. ignatianspirituality.com/ignatian-prayer/the-examen/ rummaging-for-god-praying-backward-through-your-day/).

I block out two weeks for Magdalene's story, two more for ours. The questions are on the table: Where did I come from? What did I want? What did I get? What did I lose? Even attempting to answer these will push us to a new level of intimacy, and I'm not sure we're ready, but the ladies have chosen to do their storytelling together, so I will think of them as confident Rebekahs. These questions came to me on a morning walk as I felt my mind, as it often does these days, reaching out to Lydia Roper, "What did you want? What did you get?" Without a story, she seems not to exist. At the Lydia Roper Home we may just be telling stories around the campfire, but we are here. Where is Lydia?

Sometime between the second and fourth centuries, someone buried fragments of papyrus scrolls in a jar in upper Egypt. They were discovered there by "an Arab peasant" in 1945. A portion of what is on those scrolls is known as the Gnostic Gospels, and one of those is the Gospel of Philip. In her landmark volume, *The Gnostic Gospels*, Princeton theologian Elaine Pagels translates, "the companion of the [Savior is] Mary Magdalene. [But Christ loved] her more than [all] the disciples, and used to kiss her [often] on her [mouth]". Out of this and similar translations of a fragmented scroll came the popular theory that Jesus and Mary Magdalene were married. It is the basis of centuries of religious art and even of twentieth century popular literature like *The Da Vinci Code*. It's not a particularly reputable theory, but it persists. Possibly it has its own eccentric appeal.

Do not hold onto me
(John 20:17)

Mary, called Magdalene, appears in over a dozen passages in the Gospels. In eight of those passages, she is with a group of women. With one exception, she is the first listed, clearly a leader. In the passages where she is alone, she is involved with Jesus, either at his death or at his Resurrection. Ideas about Mary Magdalene hold a large place in the Christian imagination. She is worth the time it will take us to have a look. I will send the ladies home with a question, "What do you know, or think you know, about Mary Magdalene?" After that, we will see what the Scriptures can tell us. We will read the story.

❦

Today is Wednesday the ninth of July 2014 and, with the schedule altered to include Mary Magdalene, we decide to pause where we are in our study of Acts, coming back to it in four weeks. We agree to tell Magdalene's story first, and then our own. That puts us at a bit of a loose end today, and we dabble in questions left over from last week and in some speculation about Lydia Roper.

Terry says, "She had six children; she has to be somewhere!"

The final question on the table last week was whether prayers not offered "in the name of Jesus" are heard and effective.

Today, Catherine isn't her usual confident self; she says she's not sure she has an answer.

Terry contributes her certainty that "a prayer is a prayer."

Catherine chimes in again. She has her answer: before Jesus there were a lot of people living under the law of Moses and they were all praying and their prayers were received; it's only after Jesus is resurrected that the game changes and it becomes necessary to pray in his name.

Kate reminds us that even when we're praying in Jesus' name, sometimes God's answer to a prayer is, "No."

And before we can get away, Kate has "just one more" question: "What do think it means to say we are 'saved'?"

I promise to think about it and also to ask two of my clergy friends what they think.

Nan says salvation means believing in Jesus and the Trinity and being "good, kind, considerate, and understanding ... and you'll go to heaven."

Terry: "We're saved through the grace of God."

Catherine, on the specific question of salvation by faith or good works, a subject we will revisit in depth when we get back to Acts and then to Paul's Letters, "When you have faith in Jesus, you are led by the Holy Spirit and you will just do good works."

Finally, back to Kate, with another question about salvation. "Does it mean everyone has to have an experience like Paul's? And how will I know if I'm saved? "

We recall one of our discussions about the Gospels in which we noted how often physical health and spiritual health are equated. One of my favorites is the story about the paralytic who is lowered through the roof to be healed by Jesus, who says to him not, "You are healed," but rather, "Your sins are forgiven."

I send two emails with Kate's question: what does it mean to be saved?

From the Episcopal priest comes this: "Salvation is, of course, connected in English to salve and healing. In Hebrew it is also connected with Shalom/wholeness and is also related to the word that becomes the names Joshua and Jesus ... In fact, when these words show up in the original languages they are sometimes translated into English as 'salvation' and sometimes as 'healing.' So this is at the heart of our connection with God and becoming whole people through God."

Being saved is being healed; being saved means being well.

———※⊙※———

I'm waiting to hear from my Baptist preacher.

And on Thursday, when he comes by, just back from a painful week with parents, tired from too many church demands, frustrated by a minor conflict with parishioners, for a few minutes too distracted even to begin our monthly Book-Club-of-Two discussion of *Middlemarch*, he responds: "I would rather say, 'I am being saved; I continue to be saved' than 'I am saved.' We are always in the process of being saved, with small, obvious things, even as ordinary as food. When God delivered the Israelites from bondage in Egypt and led them out through the parting sea, it was an important big salvation. When he fed them manna in the desert for forty years, it was an equally important, but less dramatic, salvation. Whatever it is, salvation is God's, not mine."

Being saved comes every day in small increments, in the middle of our lives.

———※⊙※———

There are days now when I am not sure I even have a life outside this tight container of the ladies at the Lydia Roper Home, the Bible, and all those Ropers, living and dead, found and not found. I am looking for Lydia every day, and I am not finding her. I am finding tiny glimpses, like "Liddy," which may be only a census taker's mistake; the plaque that says she increased the endowment to the Lydia Roper Home after her husband died; a former administrator's memory, based on something she heard, that the Home was probably Lydia's idea because she knew a few poor widows; a census that locates daughter Margaret's birth in Philadelphia rather than Norfolk. Each of these fragments of answers raises more questions. I am not finding Lydia.

For a while I will have to be content looking for Mary Magdalene. Her sins were forgiven, her demons cast out; she followed something she believed. She was most likely dusty, footsore, tired. Was she a young woman? Strong? Did her faith wake her with good health every morning? Was she beautiful really? It is easy to understand the temptation to which many readers of the Bible have succumbed over the years, to equate Mary with the nameless sinner with the alabaster jar who washes Jesus' feet with her hair. There is a feeling reality about them both, that they are women who have been chiseled by life, who have suffered with their heads up. There is absolutely no evidence for making that connection, but it is the source of the popular belief about Magdalene, that she was a prostitute. I also find commentary in which her seven demons have been translated into the *Seven Deadly Sins*, of all of which she is guilty.

***

Tomorrow is Wednesday July 14, and I have a small mission. Most often when I arrive early, I sit in the chairs outside the dining room or head up to Nan's room to visit. Tomorrow, I want to talk with Kate, so I will knock on her door. I want to ask her if she would be willing for me to have her son's address and phone number. I've been thinking all week that I would like to contact him to say some things that perhaps sons don't hear often enough about their mothers. I'd like him to know about Kate as I have gotten to know her at the Lydia Roper Home, about the change I have seen in her, about the enormous force for good she is in the Bible Study, about how smart she is, and sassy, and how fearless in her questions, about how she really leads the group. I'd like to say just how wonderful I think she is.

Thinking about Kate has reminded me of a story from the sixteenth century Jewish mystic, Isaac Luria. It's a creation myth and it begins when God says, "Let there be light." That light fills the void and the ten holy vessels that have appeared to carry it. The vessels embark. When they land, they will create a perfect world. Unfortunately, either God has overestimated the strength of His containers, or once again failed to understand the power of His own emanations. In any case, the vessels shatter and pieces of that heavenly light tumble, fall away, landing here and there, mostly hidden from view. The world is created an imperfect globe with holiness behind every bush. According to Luria's story, our purpose is to find and gather those sparks of God's light until enough of them are collected and the world can be restored. We do this by studying Scripture, praying, and doing good. The Hebrew words for this healing are *tikkun olam*, which means "the restoration of the world." I believe we come together on Wednesday mornings to do our share of gathering (Annie Dillard *For the Time Being* and https://www.tikkun. org/nextgen/how-the-ari-created-a-myth-and-transformed-judaism).

The nineteenth century poet William Blake wrote, "Everything that lives is holy."

I remember the moment I knew I wanted to keep bees. I was living in a large apartment that encompassed the first floor of a historic building in Louisville, Kentucky. It was an urban setting. My landlord, who lived on the third floor, had two beehives that sat right under my living room windows. Every afternoon, when the sun hit those windows, the bees would fly up into the light, looking like tiny sparks of light themselves. Soon I had a full suit of beekeeper's clothes, with long beautiful leather gloves and a veiled helmet that swathed my face and neck in protective netting. Fortunately, I was as taken with the bees as I was with the outfit. Later that year I moved to the country and set up my own small colony, five hives on a hillside that caught the afternoon sun. For a while, I had my own gathering of divine light.

I arrive early again, half an hour before the chime sounds and the doors open for breakfast. The chimes are actually an antique xylophone, mounted on the wall, with a small hammer attached for striking the keys. When a meal is on the table at the Roper Home, someone comes from the kitchen to make the musical announcement. You can hear those morning notes all through the first floor, where by then nearly everyone has gathered. Part of the morning experience at the Roper Home is listening for the mood of whoever is striking the keys.

Occasionally, when everyone seems to be smiling, a resident will take charge of the hammer and bang out her own statement for the day. Of course, I think about the old Peter, Paul, and Mary song. I had just turned seventeen the year that song appeared on my horizon. I was a freshman in college, arrived in the city from the deep woods outside a town with a population of ten thousand, blinded by what seemed unlimited possibilities where before I had seen none.

A friend recently challenged me about the questions I'm asking the ladies at Lydia Roper to address: What did you want? What did you get? She thinks they demand too much, are disturbing. She said that she would react badly to them. I thought about it. Everything we have done this year has in some way led us to this place and these questions—questions to elicit stories, questions that will reveal and try the "spiritual sinew" that ties us to each other, to the women in the Bible, to Lydia Roper, teaching her Sunday School class at Epworth Methodist Church, and to God. No, I don't think the questions ask too much. I believe it is just such questions—questions that demand, questions that intrude, uncomfortable questions just like these—that have saved us, that have healed us, that have made a space for the miracle, in this Year of our Lord 2014, in this old building named for a woman named Lydia Roper. I believe passionately that there is no more important time of life to be making demands and asking questions, to be shaking ourselves awake. Jesus warns us, "Therefore, keep awake—for you do not know when the master of the house will come, in the evening, or at midnight, or when the rooster crows, or in the morning"(Matt 13:35). We have so little time. How can we not be using it to stretch our minds as far as they will reach? We have so little to lose. I always wonder at the idea that we must be very careful with older people, must be sure they don't take unnecessary risks or become agitated. What finer time for risks and agitation and lots of outrageous questions?

Perhaps I will bring a cake for Mary Magdalene's Feast Day.

Today we will begin with the outline on Mary Magdalene. Usually, each character, book, or story requires two full handouts: an introduction and a selection of passages from the text. For Magdalene, we will manage with one. The information that would introduce her is sketchy. The passages that describe her, short. I want us to meet her where she is, through the reflective reading of Scripture that is *lectio divina* and with the help of the spiritual exercises of Saint Ignatius Loyola. I want us to hear the passages repeated. I want us, as we have before, to experience the story before we discuss the story.

Stories are meant to be heard and felt. One of my fondest memories from childhood is my father's reading to me at night. I only wanted to hear one book, an old volume of Rudyard Kipling's *The Jungle Books*. We lived on two hundred acres of North Georgia woods, and my fantasy life consisted almost entirely of becoming Mowgli, the child raised by wolves, the child whose best friends, Baloo and Bagheera, were a great brown bear and a sleek and dangerous black panther. I read "Rikki-Tikki-Tavi" and I longed for a mongoose. I remember very little about my father, a kind but distant man who died when I was sixteen, but I can still hear his voice, half a century later, reading those stories.

We will begin by finding out what we need to know about Mary, then we will walk with her, passage by passage, in her brief appearances in the Scriptures. We have never tried the *lectio divina*, and it's been a while since we practiced Ignatian Reflection with the prodigal son and the woman with the alabaster jar. As always, we choose our comfortable chairs in the second floor parlor with the Williamsburg blue furniture, crowded just a bit among the familiar faces.

⁂

In the Bible Study, our numbers are down. Wilma is gone, but for the last two weeks Cora Mae has been here. Cora Mae came to the Roper Home after I had left, and I've not found it easy to get to know her. She is wonderful to look at, tiny, dressed in layers of tops and sweaters in shimmering colors. Cora Mae is exotic, and she is dressed for travel. She carries many of her belongings in large bags, and these, too, are patchworks of colors and textures. Like the Israelites as they prepare to leave Egypt, she has her "robe girded up" and her staff in her hand. I have watched and waited for a chance.

Cora Mae is not someone you just approach; she's skittish. One day a couple of months ago, I went out to the porch to wait for my ride and Cora Mae joined me. She talked without pause.

If I listened carefully I heard the ideas she was trying so hard to push through. Cora Mae has things to say, and she wants conversation. She talked that day about siblings without names, about parents who raised her, parents who abandoned her, parents whose names she didn't know. She talked about children she had and about children she wanted but didn't have, about nameless friends from unidentified times and places; she talked about reading, about the importance of good values and a good education, about coming to Norfolk to get a job and better herself. Then she changed direction and told me she grew up here. Since that day on the porch, she has showed up for Bible Study a few times but until last month has never made it past the door where she would hover for a while, looking in. I would notice her early, then when I glanced up again, she would be gone. A few times, she came back and took up her position a second time. Twice she actually came in and sat down, but she left before we started. She was never there for more than five minutes.

During these two weeks that she's stayed with us, her speech pattern is the same as it was on the porch—the uninterrupted stream of words, the apparently incoherent stories. I am beginning to believe that we are hearing Cora Mae sorting ideas. Listen hard. Cora Mae is going through her store of thoughts and details, trying each one out, modeling them like clothes, scarf after scarf, blouse after blouse, discarding those that don't fit, finally finding the right one. It's not really much different than Evelyn looking through her boxes of earrings, trying on each pair, finding the right ones for the day. Suddenly, in the midst of today's talking, I hear one sentence, separate from all the others, that is a direct response to something Neal said a few minutes ago. Cora Mae has been here all along.

Today, she announces that she is seventy-eight. We're waiting for Inez and Catherine, in no hurry at all to break up this time. Today, Cora Mae says, her voice louder than usual, "Now I think I belong here; it's all right for me to come. It started on the porch." She remembers.

I can only say, "Cora Mae, you belong here." She smiles and is quiet.

A month ago, Cora Mae walked out the front door of the Roper Home and was gone for a whole day. The police finally found her, two blocks away, sitting on someone's front porch.

There's some shuffling around as we settle in, and the usual chatter before we start.

Now everyone is laughing at Nan and me, as Nan keeps jumping up to pass out the outlines and I keep stopping her, "Not yet; not yet."

First we will talk about Mary, called Magdalene. What are our immediate associations with her name? When we hear it, what are the very first words that come to mind?

Inez says without hesitation, "She was at the cross."

Several people chime in with, "She recognized Jesus."

Catherine asks a question that leads us to the misconceptions about Mary. "Didn't she wash Jesus' feet?"

So, we begin by examining a few of the stories that aren't true: Mary Magdalene was the unnamed woman with the alabaster jar; Mary Magdalene was Mary of Bethany, the woman in John's Gospel who also washes Jesus' feet; Mary Magdalene was a prostitute; Mary Magdalene was Jesus' wife. Getting ideas like this out of the way is one of the things that makes the introductory outlines useful; it is the first level of the reading of the text.

Finally, I give Nan the nod. At some point, a young woman who is working this summer as an intern has come in and sat in the empty seat on the sofa next to Nan. Nan has gotten pretty possessive about those handouts. Once I simply forgot and started handing them around and she joked that I was trying to steal her job. Today, for the first time ever, she turns it over and our intern passes them around.

I read aloud: "Many women were there, watching from a distance. They had followed Jesus from Galilee to care for his needs. Among whom were Mary Magdalene and Mary the mother of James and Joseph and the mother of the sons of Zebedee" (Matt 27:55-56).

The question for the first reading in the *lectio divina (sacred reading)* is "What word or image catches your attention?" This question should elicit a quick, immediate response, and today it does exactly that.

Inez steps in with, "Zebedee! I like the way it sounds." Zebedee is identified in all four Gospels as the father of James and John, two of the disciples. In both Matthew and Mark, he is left "with the hired men" in the boat after Jesus calls his sons.

And again Inez, "at a distance."

We think about that group of women, having followed closely all the way, suddenly struck by the awful importance of what is happening, stopping short of the cross, to watch. Those women, even after their years of intimacy with Jesus on the road, are afraid at the end. And this time no angel there to tell them not to be.

When Moses approaches the burning bush, God calls to him, "Come no closer! Remove the sandals from your feet, for the place on which you are standing is holy ground"(Ex. 3:5).

Kate is taken by the idea of the women who followed Jesus "to care for his needs." Inez, once a nurse, agrees.

We can't avoid a look back at the women in all the Gospels who stay when the disciples run, who understand when the disciples are confused, who accept what they can't understand, when the disciples question and doubt. And here is the Magdalene, always present.

The question for the second reading of the *lectio divina* is "What is this passage saying?" I find these responses especially intriguing; it's always been a difficult question for me.

Nan thinks it is saying that the women were "there for him." Catherine hears a promise: "They were expecting something to happen."

The process takes us then one step further toward the personal, with the question, "What is the passage saying to me, today?"

Catherine thinks the story is reminding her that she is part of the human race and that we all have to take care of each other. I know, from long hours with Catherine when I lived here, that she often feels separate, not quite connected, so what she is hearing in this story of Mary Magdalene is vital. This is what we are doing here, week after week. We are finding ourselves in these stories and we are finding these stories in our lives.

The passage says to Terry, "Have faith and I will get you through. Your name is in his Book."

In the Book of Exodus, the Book of Life contains the names of those who are "righteous before God," and in the Revelation to John, the Book is mentioned six times and lists the names of those who are "saved" by their belief in Jesus.

Kate thinks this passage, because of its catalogue of specific names, is reassuring her that we are not nameless.

For all my searching, Lydia Roper's name doesn't seem to be inscribed in anyone's book.

I read a fourth and final time as we consider the last question: "What is the passage calling me to do today?" I remind them this needs to be specific, personal, limited to this day in our lives.

And Terry's friend, Carmen, says, "To take care of myself."

Neal hears, "Help one another."

Cora Mae struggles with her drawer full of ideas and is sure that it is telling her exactly "what God wants from me ... to learn new things."

Lucille, her chin barely visible above a bright yellow blanket, says she is called by the passage to "carry forth His Glory."

Nan reminds us of Lucille's great skill, which is spontaneous prayer, "The Roper Band came in and Lucille said a prayer for them before they played. No one had ever prayed for them before." We return, briefly, to our old subject of prayer. The consensus is that it works.

⚘

By the end of the day, I find myself in temporary possession of a most remarkable item—an album of photographs, stories, poems, and small essays, assembled by a group of young people spending a summer on the New Jersey shore.

Its handmade cover is crumbling; its pages are loose. I am almost afraid to touch it.

They have come there from Philadelphia, and from New York, and from as far south as Virginia. The album is dated 1894 by its editor, Margaret Bowen Roper, oldest child of John and Lydia Roper of Norfolk. It contains, in the first few pages, a poem that is signed, "Virginia Roper." Margaret was twenty-eight that year; Ginny, only twenty-one.

A Summer-time Medley promises "Poems, Prose, and Poses."

Stories and poems by the Roper sisters are scattered throughout.

The girls are accompanied by their brothers, Albert and George, who have also contributed to this literary record of the summer.

One of the first photographs in the album, titled "A Few of 'Our Crowd' Resting at Allaire," shows a group of eight, carefully arranged on a hillside against the ruin of the Howell Ironworks in what was, earlier in the century, a thriving industrial community. In the front row is a young woman, in partial profile, dark hair piled high, dressed in the gored skirt and mutton sleeves of the period; she is looking down at a book. She catches the eye immediately, because of her central position in the photograph, because of her attention to the book rather than the camera, and because she is breathtakingly beautiful.

In the living room at the Lydia Roper Home, full of light and, incongruously, a large flat screen television, two portraits hang. One is of Lydia: she is white-haired and stately, dressed in black with a small lace fichu at the neck of her dress. Her dark eyes are soft, and there is a slight smile on her lips. Next to her is a matching portrait of John Roper, in black tie, blue eyes staring ahead under an oddly furrowed brow. The Captain is frowning. His hair and neat Van Dyke beard are a little yellowed, and it's hard to tell whether they are white or blond. Perhaps the colors have just faded. Both are thought to be the work of Adele Williams.

This painting is the only likeness of Lydia Roper I have seen.

The album, an unexpected pleasure that has suspended most of my other occupations, produces magic on every page. I am plunged into late nineteenth century America. In the very first prose piece, "A Glimpse of Our Cottage Life at Ocean Grove," the young writer describes her arrival after a long trip from Virginia: "When I reached the station ... there were any number of swell turn-outs, electric-cars, and a crowd of people moving in every direction ... After a few minutes' chat, I was taken to a cozy and sweet room to make myself presentable." Her expectation had been of "a few cottages ... no stores, one or two drives, perhaps a forest, some tents scattered about for religious services, and a great deal of water."

Founded in 1869 as part of the tent revival movement of the post-Civil War period, Ocean Grove soon became the preferred summer destination for prominent Methodist families. For a while it was even popular among tourists. At one time, there were more than six hundred tents for families attending the revivals. In 1894, the construction of the Great Auditorium had just been completed, and the New York and Long Branch Railroad was filled with visitors. The original families settled in and began to build the imposing homes that still stand today, one of which provides the setting for the first photograph in the album, "On the Porch." Summering at Ocean Grove became an established event (http://en.wikipedia.org/wiki/Ocean_ Grove,_New_Jersey), (http://kidsunplugged.org/2014/06/20/ victorian-seashore-charm-visiting-ocean-grove-new-jersey/).

We know for certain that the parents of Margaret and Ginny Roper were influential Methodists in Virginia and that they had connections in Philadelphia; Lydia might still have had family there. This summer excursion for their children would have provided a suitable retreat among other Methodist families and a sure means of maintaining those Pennsylvania connections. We have no idea whether the young Ropers ever returned to Ocean Grove.

In *A Summer-time Medley* there are only the vaguest hints as to the nature of their summer retreat. As far as we can tell, their days are not organized around attendance at revivals. At least, religious services are not something Miss Margaret Roper was inclined to include in the volume she edited in those delicious summer months of 1894. The album's narrative, verbal and photographic, sketches a lively history of the time and the particular place as the Ropers arrive at the station. On the Internet, there is a picture of a revival at Ocean Grove in 1876; there are pictures of the revival tents at today's Ocean Grove, and there is a photograph of the North End Hotel, demolished in 1980.

Never flagging, our essayist dives into the first evening's entertainment, which included a "moonlight drive," offering a view of "the lake filled with picturesque launches, lighted by the most beautiful lanterns." The ensuing days saw "our crowd" driving to the beach, swimming, visiting "the different Resorts," picnicking, playing games, and going on "a camera tour." There is a photograph in the album—"Taking the Takers"—which shows two photographers caught in the act of taking photographs. It is accompanied by a witty piece of prose describing the struggles of capturing the "takers" on film.

" TAKING THE TAKERS' "

In 1894, the Boardwalk already stretched between the religious community of Ocean Grove and the Ferris wheels and ice cream parlors of Asbury Park.

For as long as I turn the pages, I have a glimpse of a different world.

Above all, another window has opened toward Lydia, for I see her daughters in these pages: Margaret, editor and wit; Virginia, a poet, always holding a book and looking down. I now know what Ginny Roper looked like at the age of twenty-one, her life just beginning, her outlook unclouded.

I am closer; I am one generation away. I am not there.

⁂

Two days ago, Evelyn told me that her chronic eye inflammations are something more serious and may involve surgery. Her daughter, Carolyn, elaborates: Evelyn's doctors have advised against her having general anesthesia. Whatever happens, she will lose almost all her remaining eyesight.

Already, she can barely make out faces across the table, and she can't distinguish colors. She is going to be blind, and she is afraid. Already, her hearing is nearly gone, and she refuses to wear her hearing aids. What will happen when she can't see at all? I have agreed with Carolyn that, after medical decisions have been made, I'll start coming to the Roper Home an extra day a week, to spend a couple of hours with Evelyn. Carolyn says she would like me to help her mother choose outfits that match and lay them out for the week ahead. Perhaps we really are saved every day by the small things.

Today, as always, we're a little late getting started; we're waiting for Inez, who needs extra time, and figuring out that Catherine has a doctor's appointment and Cora Mae is out with her family. There's the usual chatter. Everybody knows that next week we're scheduled to start telling our own stories.

Kate is enthusiastic and is for a moment her most vivid self.

But I have seen Kate getting tired. I'm aware today that she is trying harder to come up with questions that meet some standard she's set for herself. When I ask about her experience of Magdalene's story, she hesitates, "Let me think about it for a while." Just briefly, her face falls; she looks embarrassed. I watch her tighten her grip on this woman she has become. Of all of us, Kate is the one who knows best exactly what has happened here in this circle of women in this time and place. She knows how great the change has been. She has named the exact details of her own transformation. Does that awareness of how much will be lost make this waning of energy all the more terrible? For the first time, she has to struggle to maintain it. For the last two weeks, Kate has done something she has never done once, in over a year. She has fallen asleep toward the end of the Bible Study. I understand that this aging is natural and inevitable. I am very angry about it.

Someone asks how old I was when my son was born. I say almost twenty-five: "You couldn't have gotten into too much trouble by that age." It's a good moment, relaxed, filled with easy kidding and laughter.

For a minute, I can't respond. I had more trouble than I want to remember before my son was born. I hope that I'm really not asking too much of us. I recover and pass it off with, "Oh, you'd be surprised how much trouble I found to get into!"

I escape into the work; I read aloud:

"But Mary stood weeping outside the tomb, and as she wept she stooped to look into the tomb. And she saw two angels in white, sitting where the body of Jesus had lain, one at the head and one at the feet. They said to her, 'Woman, why are you weeping? ' She said to them, 'They have taken away my Lord, and I do not know where they have laid him.' Having said this, she turned around and saw Jesus standing, but she did not know that it was Jesus. Jesus said to her, 'Woman, why are you weeping? Whom are you seeking?' Supposing him to be the gardener, she said to him, 'Sir, if you have carried him away, tell me where you have laid him, and I will take him away.' Jesus said to her, 'Mary.' She turned and said to him in Aramaic, 'Rabboni!' (which means teacher). Jesus said to her, 'Do not cling to me, for I have not yet ascended to the Father; but go to my brothers and say to them, 'I am ascending to my Father and your Father, to my God and your God.' Mary Magdalene went and announced to the disciples, 'I have seen the Lord!'" (John 20:1-18).

Back on somewhat familiar ground, we review the process of Ignatian Reflection. This morning, I opened the book I'm reading and found myself looking at a practical suggestion: What do I see? What do I hear? What do I smell? I generally have a hard time with this kind of imaginative exercise, so specific guidance like this helps me. I read the passage aloud again, then we discuss the reflection. Will we be Mary or one of the angels or Jesus? Will we be invisible observers of them all? I remember when we tried this with the Parable of the Prodigal Son. I asked, "What did you get from approaching a passage this way rather than just discussing what it means?" The unanimous answer, "We got the feelings." I read the passage again. I ask everyone to close their eyes, and I read it a final time, then allow a few minutes of silence.

The questions: What did I experience, as that character, in this story? What did I see? What did I hear? What did I smell? What did I feel?

Nan speaks up right away and goes directly to the hardest question. "I was Mary and I felt afraid and confused and sad.

He was dead and I didn't understand that and I couldn't find the body. I felt afraid."

My friend, Betsy, who is here today because she's been reading about these ladies and wanted to meet them, says, "If it were me, I'd have taken one look at those angels and high-tailed it out of there. Wouldn't they have been scared to death of two big white angels, probably with wings? "

And we stop to tell Betsy about our reading of all the resurrection stories and the refrain, "Do not be afraid." In first century Palestine the lines between the natural and the supernatural were not firm like in today's world. We obviously can't know whether people saw angels. What we do know is that someone felt comfortable writing about angels without making them unusual. The readers of that story were clearly expected to take them in stride.

Carmen is back today and she has taken all the questions seriously: "Mary sees the open tomb; she has to stoop to look in; then she sees the angels sitting where Jesus' body should be; it takes her a minute to understand what she's looking at; she is smelling the spices that she's brought to anoint the body. She is not afraid of angels; her concern is finding Jesus."

As I listen to Carmen's description of the scene, I realize that I am present in that scene in a more vivid and concrete way than ever before. By actually paying attention to these small sensory details, Carmen has brought everything and everyone into focus. She has frozen the moment in time and I am not just thinking about what it might have been like; I am seeing, smelling, touching along with Mary. Carmen's second day with us has turned into a lesson in reading and teaching for me.

Terry says, "Mary is feeling alone, beaten down, confused, just trying to stay on her feet."

The Magdalene is at the end of her rope here. Jesus is dead; the body is lost; this gardener is the only person around. We think she's probably just wishing she could go home.

We remember the speculation about Mary's relationship with Jesus. After dismissing again the idea that she was Jesus' wife, we still recognize that this was a strong relationship of some kind; these two loved each other. I think Carmen is right in her perception—Mary is distraught because her "Lord" is gone, not just dead, but the body lost; she's not looking at much else. This man has been the focus of her life for at least two years; she has walked the roads with him every day. She has believed in him; he has healed her of seven demons. Whatever they were, those "demons" must have ravaged her. Because of Jesus, she is well. He's dead, and now she can't find his body, can't think what to do with this ointment she's prepared. She leaves the tomb, not quite knowing where to go next. She turns, and there is someone she can ask.

Betsy brings up another question we've touched on before. Why doesn't Mary recognize Jesus? We recall, in particular, the story of the two disciples who walked with Jesus on the road to Emmaus and failed to recognize him. We recognize Jesus only when we are ready. In this case, though, who knows if Mary is ready or not? She has no experience of anything like resurrection. Why would she connect her dead Lord with this man standing behind her near the tomb?

We talk, of course, about names. I ask, "What happens that makes her recognize him? What does he say to her? "Mary." He says nothing more than her name, and we know about names. Here, it's all that's required: "Mary." And her response, "Rabbi." Names are important; names matter.

I move us into the preparation for next week; I hand out papers with the four questions: Where did I come from? What did I want? What did I get? What did I lose? We have run out of women, run out of stories; we are simply next in line. We will now begin to search for our own stories as we are searching for Lydia's. I go over the catalogue of stories to date. It always ends up back at us.

I talk about Lydia and how I "wrote" these questions by wondering what I would ask her if I could.

I am almost certain I know what the answers would be for Jack Roper. He came from a hardscrabble youth in a backwoods town in Pennsylvania, a half-orphan nearly from birth, raised by his mother, who had two other children. He was most likely apprenticed when he was around thirteen to work in the general store; at twenty-one he left for California to mine for gold then signed up for the War as soon as he came home. Jack Roper wanted wealth and position; he wanted respectability. And he got it all. The Ropers are one of the most highly respected families in Norfolk. And John Lonsdale Roper accomplished that. We can't know what he lost.

Lydia was twenty-five when she married Captain John Roper. She was a spinster. There is very little information about her family in Philadelphia, and there are no stories. Lydia left that life, whatever it was. What did she want? What did she get?

I don't know.

"She wanted love. She just loved Jack. He was adventurous; maybe she needed a change."

Kate muses about the portrait of Lydia Roper in the downstairs living room, "I don't know why, but she looks like she'd be tall." I remark that someone in the family told me that Jack Roper was short.

There's not much left to say. I talk about the questions and ask us all to think them over. We'll start next Wednesday with the first question, "Where did I come from?"

Maybe next week we can begin to ask ourselves what we feel in our own stories. At this minute I realize fully what a difficult question that is: what do I feel as I tell my story? If I take this seriously, I guess I will find out. We are about to add our stories to all the stories we have read, to all the stories we have heard, to all the stories we have imagined. How brave will we be?

We have these catalogues, of which we will now make ourselves a part:

We began with Eve and we read the stories of the women in the Hebrew Bible. The wives of the patriarchs: Sarah, Rebekkah, and Rachel; and David's wives: Michal, Abigail, Bathsheba; the prophet Deborah; the warrior Jael; the unnamed concubine, raped to death and left on the doorstep of her lover's house; David's daughter, Tamar, sent in by her father to be raped by her cousin; and what about Bathsheba? The king "sent messengers to get her" (2 Sam 11:4); Delilah; Jezebel; Ruth and Naomi. We went back to the beginning and started with Adam and we read the stories of the men in the Hebrew Bible. We read God's story.

We have read the story of Jesus of Nazareth and the stories of the women who carried him—in a womb or along the dusty roads of Galilee: the young girl, Mary, his mother; her cousin, Elizabeth; the prophet, Anna; the woman healed of a hemorrhage; Peter's mother-in-law; the women of Samaria; the women of means who supported his mission and followed him to Jerusalem; Mary Magdalene.

We have the catalogue of the women of the Roper family: Lydia Roper, the wife of the patriarch; her daughters, Margaret and Virginia; the daughters-in-law, come from New York and Philadelphia to marry Roper men—the first wives, Georgiana and Isabelle; and the second wives, Maida and Ethel; Adele Williams; and, of course, John Roper's mother, Esther. We have stories about them all. We know that Margaret was a social activist who helped found shelters for women and a hospital for poor children; we know that Ginny was a musician and composer. We know she was beautiful; we have heard that Georgette buggy-whipped a man and we know that she published stories under the name George Phillips; we know that Maida exhibited her paintings in Italy and in France, that Adele Williams was the artist chosen to paint most of the Roper family portraits and that she had a studio in their home in the Pennsylvania mountains. These women are becoming real to me. They exist in their stories; they are alive in their stories. Hearing their stories, I can imagine them. I can imagine them just as I imagine Mary Magdalene or the prodigal son or the woman washing Jesus' feet with her tears, just as I can conjure Rebekkah or Hagar or Bathsheba. They belong to me because I know their stories. I don't have to imagine the women at the Lydia Roper Home; I see them every week.

Very soon I will know their stories.

I cannot see Lydia's face at all. I cannot imagine her. I do not know her story.

Chapter Five

PRELIMINARIES
CATHERINE

CATHERINE IS SURE THAT we were reading books together before the Bible Study ever started. She can tell me which books we read and exactly when I stopped coming; she is sure it was when I started the Bible Study. She makes it clear that she was not happy about it, that she feels I left our reading in favor of the women in the Bible Study. This is something we will work out. She has an exact date in mind for her arrival at the Lydia Roper Home.

She moved into her room on April 3, 2013. I find my own date. I walked through the doors of the Roper Home on February 21, 2013. I had just passed my sixty-seventh birthday. In those circumstances, time distorts. It seems both longer ago and dangerously close. I left the Lydia Roper Home on October 31, 2013. That afternoon, a good friend's ninety-year-old father died. I left this co-op piled high with boxes and spent Halloween weekend with her. On another All Saints' Day, twenty years ago, I took my mother's ashes to North Georgia and dug them into the dirt on my father's grave. There were bone chips in the ashes, and I could feel the grit on my skin. My hands smelled of smoke.

Catherine is ninety-seven. She was born in Norfolk, grew up in Norfolk, got her education in Norfolk, taught in Norfolk, married three times and buried three husbands in Norfolk, lived through the Civil Rights years and the integration of the Norfolk schools.

When Catherine and I were reading together, we always read her books, and we read whatever she picked out. There were books on Michelangelo, on ancient Greece and on ancient Rome; I think there was a museum book of religious art, and there was a book about ancient Israel. We read in a tiny sitting room on the third floor. We also spent long stretches of time in Catherine's room, while she told me stories about her life and I took notes, wishing for a tape recorder. Finally, her nephew brought her a small tape deck, but we couldn't get it to work; after several days' struggles I discovered that it wasn't plugged in! We did manage to record about an hour of Catherine's often hilarious tales of her grandmother's maxims and their fame in the family--even when they made so little sense that Catherine and I were reduced to helpless laughter. Ultimately, I relied on my notes. I typed up a manuscript and printed a copy for Catherine; when I bought this new laptop in December, the digital file was lost. Catherine can't find hers.

On the day when Catherine would have talked about her life, I am at breakfast and she tells me she is leaving the Lydia Roper Home and will be gone by the end of the month. I am horrified, and I show it. She is surprised and pleased that I care. I don't want to lose her. She tells me defiantly that she knows "your friends don't like me." She is an intriguing mix of aggressive self-confidence and paralyzing uncertainties. Today she announces that she was the first "African" at Lydia Roper, then she looks around to say, "Then Neal came; and Lucille." Catherine is very alert to racial matters. I can remember her talking about this when we got together to read, and about her involvement in the integration of the schools in Norfolk. She is angry. It isn't something that is resolved in her mind. It isn't something that is resolved in the world, and Catherine knows it. She doesn't want anyone to forget.

Since early days, Catherine, who never sits on the fence about anything, has shifted between two strong opinions about the Bible Study. On the one hand, she has taken enthusiastically to all the new information. She loves learning and has never had this kind of background and analysis of the Bible. Like several of the ladies, the only time Catherine has heard someone talk about the Bible is as part of a sermon. I'm afraid there aren't any sermons on our Wednesday mornings; we have discovered that most of the questions don't have answers, that asking the questions connects us to God, that listening to each other as we grapple with the questions leads us directly toward the Divine. Catherine thrives on this exploration.

On the other hand, she has turned out to be a fiery preacher, and I have been the primary target of her sermons. She has told me forcefully, from the first week and with a grin on her face, that God has brought me here and that God has a plan to get me to stop asking so many questions and just find the Truth. I have to confess I enjoy these sermons. Dignified Catherine has a streak of the tent revivalist in her, and it's a style of preaching to which I have always been secretly attracted. An Episcopalian from the cradle, every once in a while that good old Gospel message, delivered with enthusiasm, strikes me just the right way. I have loved Catherine's confident, sure-minded sermons, aimed at letting me know that I wasn't fooling Jesus with all this intellectual folderol. Jesus was just waiting to snatch me up.

Today, Catherine is older. For the most part, she has just slowed down, unable to exert herself to hear me or the discussions, falling asleep soon after we get started. What combination of circumstances makes this happen? Certainly the fact of being ninety-seven pulls downward. But, that's not all it is. This inexorable process of aging is profoundly depressing to some of us held captive in the grip of inertia, those of us who defined ourselves by what we did. There is no escape from these final aches and pains, the diminished stamina, and the fact of having, really, nothing we need to do. For all her certainty, Catherine is just plain tired. I want to see one more knowing look, hear one more ornery sermon, one more argument against something I've said about a Gospel or the early Church. I long for one more moment of Catherine, zealous for the welfare of my soul.

Today is also the day that Kate comes in late from her hair appointment looking pale and thin and falls asleep almost immediately; the day that Inez doesn't get to Bible Study because her legs won't support her; the day that Evelyn breaks down from fear that the doctors are going to take out her eye. Today is the day I am told that I can't take photographs of the Bible Study group as it goes against corporate policy.

Today is a day of overwhelming sadness and some deep anger for me. God just seems to be testing the ladies, one after another, and now they are being denied, for whatever good reasons, the simple pleasure of sitting down with a pile of photographs that were taken in fun, laughing at themselves and each other, having a few minutes of foolishness. Foolishness is important. This is an important loss.

Life in a group home can be difficult. I suspect, to quote Scott Peck, that "life is difficult" regardless of location. At the Lydia Roper Home, however, we are in a smaller world where all the problems and all the blessings are magnified.

Some days, I can hardly think about the Bible we have come here to read. Or I think only about those stories that disturb, like Jephthah's daughter, victim to her father's lack of faith; Hagar, victim to Yahweh's plan for His people; Tamar, victim of all the men in her family, starting with her father, King David; the woman weeping at Jesus' feet; Bathsheba, sent for by the king; Magdalene through the centuries, her reputation confused, her story lost. And how many will go back into the text to find her?

I can't know about the pain in Catherine's life. I can know her by her wounds, as she knows me by mine.

Perhaps what we all need is what Magdalene needed at the tomb: a rabbi to call us by name.

On Catherine's last day in Bible Study, she sits up straight, looks me in the eye, and begins to preach on the peril of my soul as it struggles with unnecessary questions when time is short. She even shakes her fist at the group she feels has rejected her.

This is Catherine's parting shot. She has nothing to lose now, and she is witnessing to something for which the apostles died.

Chapter Six

FACES
NAN AND TERRY

SUDDENLY, AFTER MONTHS OF searching, I have three photographs of Lydia Bowen Roper. In one, undated, she looks like a schoolgirl. The next, dated on the back, 1900, shows her at sixty. In the third, she is near eighty. Unlike the delightfully posed "casual" photographs taken by the young people at Ocean Grove in the summer of 1894, these are formal portraits. Sharply different in their portrayal of Lydia, they are alike in that one respect: they have been "sat for."

As I began to find Ropers and get to know them, the photographs started to appear. Bruce Forsberg, one of Lydia's great-granddaughters, went through boxes she says hadn't been opened in decades and sent me a large package. In that box was, among many other treasures, the photograph of Lydia and John, their son William, and a baby Elizabeth, who grew up to be Bruce's mother. The photographs of a young Lydia and of Lydia close to eighty hang on the wall of Molly Roper Jenkins' house in Lynchburg, Virginia. I have found a beautiful antique frame for the family photograph from Bruce and will return it to her, framed, when I meet her.

The first picture is full-face, head and shoulders only. It is a small picture in a small gold-leaf frame. My first sight of it is a photograph that Molly took and emailed to me. It is blurry, difficult to make out. Depending on the exact date, the photographer would possibly have still used either daguerreotype or the later tintype; he has created an effect common to those processes, a halo surrounding the subject. Lydia's dark hair, blurred around the edges, is pulled straight back from her forehead and over her ears, unadorned, without obvious style, plain, probably held with a clasp or pins, falling loosely at least past her shoulders. She is wearing a dark plaid dress or blouse, with the type of short, white, detachable collar that was a staple of women's dress in the nineteenth century. If she is, say, sixteen in this picture, the year would have been 1856. I get out my magnifying glass and my laptop. I look up nineteenth century women's hairstyles and find photograph after photograph, not of young Lydia's hairstyle, but of the same style of photography. Here are Victorian women and girls, head and shoulders suspended on pale backgrounds, edges faded. Months later, when I see the photograph for myself I will be undone by the clarity of every detail. Here, indeed, is Lydia Bowen.

I call Molly in Lynchburg. The photograph has hung there for many years and she doesn't know where it came from. She had thought it was a picture of Lydia soon after her wedding. The young Lydia's likeness now hangs near an early photograph of her future husband, probably in his twenties. Molly tells me that in the actual picture of Lydia, there is no halo. I am disappointed that what I see might be only a reflection of light on the glass. She also says that what I had taken either for Lydia's long hair, falling down her back, or her hair pulled into large loops behind her ears, is, in fact, a bow. Someone has tied Lydia's hair back with a very large ribbon.

The truth is that there's no way of knowing how old she is in this photograph. Two things are clear to me: Lydia looks undeniably like a schoolgirl. If this is a picture of Lydia as a young girl, then it must have come from Philadelphia. Stories can be deceptive. There is no provenance for this picture.

I am learning something about research. I am not learning nearly as much as I'd like about Lydia Roper. So far, the pictures raise more questions than they answer.

The young Lydia, in this photograph, is both obvious and utterly elusive. I return to her face. It isn't possible to look at this picture without noticing that Lydia Bowen has a very large nose. She isn't a beauty, but that face is compelling.

For a schoolgirl, she looks serious, a little withdrawn, her mind somewhere else. What I have is a photograph of a scanned photograph of the photograph, which is in a frame, behind glass, in another city. I know that my excitement is so high, my desire now so great to find her story in each image, that I am capable of spinning a yarn to get me by. When I look closely, I see that Lydia Bowen might also look determined or stubborn, perhaps even defiant, perhaps bored with sitting, perhaps simply a teenager. I can't know, because I have no stories. Stories are important. Pictures are important, too, but for some reason, they are not revealing Lydia. I had thought that, once I saw her face, I would know. I have seen it, at three stages of her life, and I do not know.

I have begun to know the ladies at the Lydia Roper Home. I see their faces; I hear their stories. Week by week, I have watched Nan and Terry together. Nan is the mother of Terry's best friend.

Once a week, for many months, Terry has come to the Roper
Home to spend time with Nan, to take her shopping, to take her
out to eat, just to take her out; she has blocked out a day every
week that is her day to come to Nan. Since she joined the Bible
Study, that day is Wednesday and sometimes I am included in
their afternoon. I watch them, these women of two generations,
comfortable together, accustomed to each other's small quirks,
attuned to each other's needs, keeping each other company. I
imagine Ruth and Naomi, walking the road from "the country of
Moab," where Naomi and her husband had fled from a famine, to
return, as widows, to Naomi's homeland, Bethlehem, in Judah.
That story is about famine and abundance, about isolation and
companionship. Is that what these months at the Lydia Roper
Home have been about: surviving the famine; bringing in an
unexpected harvest?

Terry has her own story of feast and famine. She gives where
she can and is one of the women who helped buy our microphone.
She takes notes for me in our Bible Study discussions; she holds
Nan up. Like Luke's Jesus she "goes around doing good." But
Terry isn't well and her days are often filled with so much pain
she can hardly manage. I see Nan's watchful eye on her. Two
women, one older and one younger. Like Ruth and Naomi and
all of us here, by some miracle, "they came to Bethlehem at the
beginning of the barley harvest" (Ruth 1:22).

Nan tells us she came from Trenton, New Jersey: "My life
growing up was just like a soap opera. Sunday church, chicken
every Sunday. My father was a bus driver and a plumber. My
mother worked in what I guess you'd call an 'elite' dress shop.
I worked first as an order clerk and liked the job, finally as a
receptionist in a doctor's office, a job I loved."

I interrupt to ask if the doctor's office was where she was
told that her voice was "too sexy" when she answered the phone.
She confesses that it was; the confession comes with a pleased,
arch smile.

"I guess what I wanted was what my parents had."

The next week, Nan adds that she "had a brother. We always
fought. He died an alcoholic. He's been gone so long he was just
out of my mind.

"I got married and was married for ten years, but didn't have any children. Then I just got up one day and decided that I didn't know what marriage was even for if you didn't have children, so we adopted two wonderful children, a boy and a girl. They were great, trouble-free kids. My son smoked grass. One time I found a bag of it in his room and threw it out. Later, one of his friends came by for it and I had to say, 'Sorry. I threw it away.'

"I married my second husband and I really liked him. He had a doctorate and he thought I was just great."

Nan and Terry make up a pair and they've got each other's backs.

Nan walked in that front door on May 16 2013. She has been here more than a year.

Chapter Seven

PIONEERS
KATE, INEZ, AND EVELYN

WE CAME TOGETHER FOR two Wednesdays to talk, not about the Scriptures, but about ourselves. Somewhere along the line, we must have decided that it's safe to do that.

Kate volunteered to be first, and she talked for a long time:

"I've thought a lot about these questions, especially where did I come from. Before my parents even thought about me, where was I? Was I with God? Then I was born. I was an only child; everyone thought I was spoiled. I did well in school and I always knew I wanted to go to college and I wanted to teach. I wanted very much to teach children in first grade. My father owned a sporting goods store, sold golf clubs, tennis rackets, guns. I want to believe that if he'd known and heard what we know today about guns, maybe he wouldn't have sold them. He sold them to people who hunted for sport. He would bring home rabbits he'd shot and my mother could hardly bear to look at them.

"Two years before I graduated from high school, the Depression hit. The business was failing and my father eventually sold the store and at fifty he got a job. This happened two years before my high school graduation and of course college was out of the question; there was no money. That was a time of terrible personal depression when I almost lost my faith. My grandfather on my mother's side paid for voice lessons for me, but I had to get to those lessons on my own. I took the bus to the ferry, then—for a nickel— the ferry across to Norfolk. From there I took another bus to Monticello Avenue, then walked to another bus stop, rode again, walked several blocks, and finally knocked on the voice teacher's front door. We had recitals, and anytime I had to sing in public, I got sick—not physically, but I felt sick. I remember the first time we had to sing and my solo was, *Little drops of water; little grains of sand ... something, something, I will make my stand.*

"Then I went to sing one Easter season at an Episcopal church. Their soloist had gotten sick and someone asked me to fill in. It was my first paid singing job. I knew nothing about the Episcopal Church—I was always a Methodist. I had two weeks to learn the whole liturgy and the cantata. After that, they asked me if I would stay permanently; I was there for eight years. I thought that maybe I wouldn't be able to teach children but could teach something with my singing in the church."

Kate had a dream. She wanted to go to college and to teach young children. She got neither. She got, instead, the voice of an angel, and a job using it. What did she want? What did she get? What did she lose? What are the compromises we make? Are they enough? Do we, perhaps, find even more than we hoped for? Kate says that sometimes, when she was supposed to sing, she just had "no song in me," and didn't know what to do about that. So she prayed and sang. Kate tells us that she never really did leave home. When she married, she and her husband moved into the house with her parents. Did that voice and that lovely mind allow her to chase her dream right where she was? In *The Path of Waiting,* Henri Nouwen says "the thing we are waiting for is growing out of the ground on which we are standing." Was Kate waiting for something? Is she waiting still? Are we all? Nouwen says that even God is waiting, waiting to see in what way we will receive him. When Jesus arrives in Jerusalem for the last time, he must wait for us to decide whether we will follow him or crucify him.

Simone Weill writes that "the essence of the spiritual life is to wait, with expectation."

Kate arrived at the Lydia Roper Home exactly twenty days before I did. We have spent all our weeks together for a year and a half. Just as we were ending our last day of storytelling, Kate looked up at me and said quietly, "I am always reluctant to leave."

✦✦✦

The second photograph I have of Lydia Roper is dated 1900. She was sixty, John, sixty-five. They are posed for a family portrait. The Captain is sitting in a Victorian armchair, his elbows resting on the arms, his hands dropping casually toward his lap. He is wearing a dark three-piece suit and a white shirt, with a bow tie tucked neatly under the collar. His hair is white, receding at the forehead. It is just possible to make out the beginnings of the chin whiskers that would become the full beard of later years. In what looks like a slipper chair next to him, his son, William, sits, holding a baby. I know that this baby is William's daughter, Elizabeth, who will grow up to be the mother of Lydia and John's great-granddaughter, Bruce, who sent this picture to me. William has his mother's nose.

In between the two men, and standing, is Lydia. She is wearing a white, or perhaps pale yellow, dress with small polka-dots. A dark ribbon encircles her waist. Fine columns of ruffles run from the round neckline to the waist and are repeated down the sides of the sleeves. The long sleeves are rucked, slightly puffed where they meet the shoulder. It is a good dress, perhaps one reserved for Sundays; it also looks like a comfortable dress. Lydia Roper looks like a comfortable woman. Judging by this photograph, she does not appear to be a woman much concerned with fashion. In most photographs of well-to-do women at the turn of the century, clothes are elaborate, hair carefully assembled; more casual hairstyles don't appear until women begin cutting their long hair. Photographs, including one of a very young Zelda Fitzgerald, look toward the age of the Flapper. Lydia's gray hair is pulled up into a twist, wisps of hair escaping on both sides and at the top. It may have taken hours to assemble in the morning, but Lydia's day has begun to pull it apart. She looks like a woman who might have been called from some work to change her dress quickly and sit for a photograph. I don't see any sign of makeup. She is looking straight ahead.

Her eyes are clear, her gaze unwavering. She looks kind, and she looks solid. I like her mouth. The arm next to her husband falls behind his shoulder. Possibly she has put her hand on the arm of his chair. Her other arm is raised and her hand is resting on her son's back. The baby charms the picture and is wearing a dress. Someone has decided that Elizabeth can pose for this picture without shoes, and we see her feet, looking uncompromisingly like a baby's feet.

What did this woman want? I have the picture of the young girl; I have this picture of the grandmother. Between the ages of twenty and sixty, no pictures have turned up, and I have no way of even guessing what those years brought or what they took away. The Lydia Roper of this family scene looks content and settled. Whatever life has demanded, she has weathered it well. Like the women at the Lydia Roper Home, she has survived. She lived another thirty years.

John L. Roper, age 65
Lydia Bowen Roper, age 60
William Roper
Elizabeth Roper

I know more about Lydia than I did because my friends at the library's local history collection have found two longer obituaries, one published on the day of her death, one the day after.

She is no longer invisible. As it turns out, she did not arrive in Norfolk and disappear. The headline on the first obituary reads, "Mrs. Lydia H. Roper Claimed by Death: Widely-Known and Beloved Norfolk Woman Long Active in Affairs of City." Both go on to say that Lydia Roper was "known for her extensive philanthropic work ... known as one of the most charitable women in the city." According to both articles, she was responsible for maintaining "a cottage at Willoughby Beach as a summer recreational home for working girls who otherwise would have been unable to enjoy seashore benefits." John Roper may have provided the money, but it was Lydia's project. She was also actively involved with hospital work, as her oldest daughter, Margaret, spearheaded the founding of the King's Daughters in Norfolk. These were active women, organized and efficient. They got things done. I first ran across that description of Ropers in an article that described the men of the Roper family as men who had "done things."

I now know that at the funeral services, held at the residence on Freemason Street, the house was full, the casket was covered "with a pall of white roses," and a quartet sang, "Faith of Our Fathers" and "Jesus, Lover of my Soul." I think of Kate and her favorites, "the stately hymns of the church."

A public Lydia Roper begins to emerge. She was known in the city. She was concerned with the needs of the poor, the sick, and the elderly. She was generous. She must have been determined, once she set her mind on something. Why am I not satisfied? What do I want? What am I chasing? In my first conversation with Bruce, almost the first thing she said was, "You're not going to find out anything about Lydia Roper. I was on the Board of the Lydia Roper Home. My mother was on the Board; my grandmother was on the Board. The only thing any of us ever heard said about Lydia Roper was that she was married to John Roper who built the Lydia Roper Home and named it for her."

There are no stories about Lydia Roper. There are no stories like the stories I have found or heard about every other member of the family; there are no stories like the ones my family delights in telling about each other. There are just no stories at all.

Molly says I can be sure of one thing: Lydia's children adored her. Toward the end of her life, Margaret called only for her "Mama."

Inez tells us again that she grew up in a small town. "I was an only child," she says, right after Kate has spoken, "I was spoiled, too. My father worked for the railroad. In 1920 the railway workers went on strike and he had to go to work in a store.

"I graduated from high school in 1941, and I knew I wanted to be a nurse. I started at the local hospital and was there a year. I had health problems and couldn't keep on with my training so I had to leave nursing. I was a medical technician for years. Then I met my husband."

Inez is more reluctant to talk in the group, and most of what I know about her life came from a long conversation we had in her room one day, months ago. Today, she kept it short, but I am interested in what she pulled from the fuller version: the strike; her father's change in employment; her health problems; her marriage.

Inez's is another story in which, as a friend of mine says, "Life just showed up." What do we lose and what do we gain when life just shows up?

I don't know how long Inez has been here; I am almost certain she was here when I arrived in February of 2013.

What did we learn from all those women in the Hebrew Bible for whom life showed up in some harsh ways? Jephthah's daughter was inside the family tent when her father, back from victory in battle, approached. She ran out to greet him. But Jephthah, not quite confident in the Spirit of God that had come to him before he went out to fight, made one last deal. If God would give him the victory, he would sacrifice the first living creature to emerge from the tent on his return. Life showed up one last time for his daughter, who asked only to be allowed to retreat with the women she knew into the mountains to "bewail her virginity."

We have been more fortunate, these women at the Lydia Roper Home and I; our losses have been less drastic, our compromises not final. We've had second chances. But, what did we want? What dreams were we chasing? These may be, like so many questions we have asked for almost two years, questions that don't have answers. Maybe we learn that not all the questions need to be answered. Maybe it's all in the asking.

Evelyn asks, "Where did I come from? I think I came from God and my parents. I had loving parents. I lost my father when I was young and my mom was left with four children to raise. When I asked her 'where I came from,' she always said I came from a big rock and for years I thought I came from a rock. She was good and raised us as good Christians." There are gaps in this story, more questions than answers. Later, holding back tears as she tries to understand what the doctors have said about her eye, Evelyn says to me, "Can I just tell the rest to you?" I will go in an extra day next week. Evelyn is leaning hard on her belief in God, but I can see her struggling to come to terms with her encroaching blindness. Jesus tells the crowd, when they assume a man's blindness is due to sin, his or his parents', that he is blind "so that God's works might be revealed in him." Is Evelyn going blind so that God's works can be revealed?

Evelyn was married twice, the first time at sixteen. Her husband was a golf pro and, according to Evelyn, an alcoholic and a womanizer. They divorced. At twenty-three, she married again. "He was in the service, and I got to travel—Spain, Guam, Washington, D.C. He was nice; he was good to me."

Evelyn tells us that she came to the Lydia Roper Home "one year and eighteen months ago."

All I know is that on the day I arrived, the Bible pioneers were there waiting for me.

Chapter Eight

THE PORTRAITS
LUCILLE, NEAL, AND CORA MAE

WE WERE IN OUR final discussion of Kate's question about Jesus and the Gentiles. Neal had never asked questions or offered comments, and she had been coming faithfully to Bible Studies every week since she arrived at Lydia Roper. Lucille had never really spoken. Her frequent interjections of "Amen!" and "Yes, Lord," were her only participation. Cora Mae wasn't with us at all yet.

That discussion was only one week before Neal did have something to say, something so profound that I wondered if she had just been waiting for the right moment. I remember I read aloud the Parable of the Prodigal Son, and Neal made her quiet admission that she was the good one who was never appreciated, that she was the one with resentments. And then she said, with total confidence, that everything in this family would turn out fine, that the younger son would realize his mistakes, the older son forgive, the father rest in the love of his small family.

This week again, as we pull up the last threads of our stories and revisit those intrusive questions, we try to recall when we arrived at the Lydia Roper Home and how we got here.

Neal reminds us about her stroke, "It wiped out everything; I've tried hard to bring something back, to remember, but it's just gone. I don't remember how I got here; I woke up one morning and I was here."

Neal said that sometimes when we're doing something really hard, we don't even see our surroundings anymore.

Neal said that the woman who washed Jesus' feet with her tears was crying "because she didn't want to be there."

Neal remembers keeping her dad's books on the farm. She remembers they grew corn and cotton and tobacco; and she remembers her red bike.

Where I find Neal, I can usually find Lucille. Often they sit in the first floor living room after breakfast, napping, television turned to a morning talk show. I wonder whether they talk to each other. Memory fails me again. I don't really know when Lucille came to the Lydia Roper Home. Many of the ladies don't remember when they came.

Of all of them, I know the least about Lucille. She almost never talks, even in those informal moments or places where nearly everybody chats about games or today's lunch menu or about the singing group scheduled to visit in the afternoon. Lucille is usually there. I don't know that I've ever seen her sitting alone. But she doesn't talk. There have been no times together on the porch and no quiet conversations before Bible Study. The more I think about Lucille, the more I realize I have never actually had a conversation with her at all. I now know that Lucille is really wonderful at extemporaneous prayers, and I have made a point of asking her to start us off with a prayer. When she prays, she is clear and articulate; she never misses a beat.

This week, as we talked about ourselves, I realized for the first time how difficult it is for Lucille to express herself. She wasn't able to do it. I guess I had never heard her try. Lucille has been here, silent, for months, and I have not gone beyond her "amens" and her prayers. I feel I have let her down somehow.

On Wednesday, I stood next to her, straining to hear; I have come home to pore over Terry's notes. There I find that Lucille told us she grew up in Norfolk; the name of the neighborhood isn't clear. She had sisters, possibly seven, possibly a brother. Now I try to remember if Lucille has visitors; I think she does. In fact, I seem to recall a few times when more than one person, maybe children, maybe nieces or nephews, came to get her from Bible Study.

I puzzle over this. Lucille, who has been present at the Bible Study since we were meeting in the big living room, who has never failed to show up, who always has a smile for me, has somehow remained invisible. And yet, at the same time, she has seemed an active part of the group. Did Lucille participate more when she first came; are my impressions of her memories from months ago? Is this silence a change that I just haven't noticed until now? She is certainly sleeping more, and has only recently started wrapping herself in a blanket. If I knew when she got here, maybe I could piece it together.

I think about the others that elude us. There are no stories for Lydia Roper, no names for the woman with the alabaster jar, the concubine in the time of the judges, the Samaritan woman at the well. Nothing about David's daughter, Tamar, after her rape by her brother; nothing about Moses' sister, Miriam, or about David's first wife, Michal, after God punishes them for challenging the men He has chosen. So very many missing details; so many missing women. As long as Lucille is here, joining us on Wednesday mornings in whatever way she can, she will not be missing.

For today, I can count on their being there in the living room—Lucille, Neal, sometimes Cora Mae—watched over by Captain John and Lydia Roper, in the portraits that Adele Williams painted, perhaps in her studio on the Blue Ridge Summit estate.

Those portraits do not loom over the space. They do not inform or control the atmosphere of the room. They are, in fact, easy to overlook, and I did overlook them for months. They aren't especially large. The focal point of the room is the large television. Once the portraits were pointed out to me, I examined them more closely, and still I am not engaged. They don't look like anyone to whom I would devote hours and days and weeks of my time. They don't look remotely like people whose history I would pursue more diligently than I've chased after my own.

Lydia looks too much like anyone's kindly grandmother and John like the grandfather whose frown could send you scampering. I wonder if Lydia Roper's portrait was taken from the photograph I've seen rather than from life. Perhaps the same is true for the Captain. Adele Williams was interested in photography and sometimes painted from photographs rather than from life.

I understand these are formal portraits painted well before 1920. I know the period dictates the style. They still seem oddly impersonal. Maybe I've been looking for John and Lydia Roper too long to be satisfied. Still, they don't reflect the delicacy of Adele Williams' watercolors of woods near Richmond or a street scene in Bermuda.

I look again at the third photograph of Lydia, which hangs, along with the first, on a wall in Lynchburg, Virginia. This is the face of a determined and lively eighty-year-old Lydia Roper. This eighty-year-old might still be visiting hospitals and talking to women in trouble. This eighty-year-old knows what she wants and hasn't yet retired from going after it.

She appears, as in the portrait at the Lydia Roper Home, kind and elderly, but she looks straight out from the photograph, insisting on your attention. I can see the woman in the portrait here, can see that, if I look more closely I might discover more in that painting. I am glad I have the photograph. She is dressed conventionally, in either lace or brocade; her hair is white, her nose still prominent. I wonder if that nose is evident in the painting; I'll have to look. I've grown quite fond of that obvious imperfection in a face otherwise unremarkable except for the steady gaze looking out from all the photographs. That gaze is something by which I do know Lydia Roper.

Cora Mae, of the colors and textures and bags of belongings, of the constant chatter that suddenly erupts into clarity, has been gone for three Wednesdays now. Everyone thinks she's with family, at some sort of reunion. No one is sure of the details. When she is here, Cora Mae's gaze is nervous, evasive, startled. She doesn't look straight ahead.

Is Cora Mae missing?

I look back over the dates I've been able to find: when we left home; when we arrived at the Lydia Roper Home. Evelyn seems to have been here the longest. Several of us arrived within a month or two of each other. Kate and I came in February; Catherine, in April; Nan, in May. Neal just can't remember, but Catherine thinks Neal got here soon after she did. I can't recall when Lucille came. Cora Mae possibly came most recently. Of course, every day now there are new women, but they are not a part of this story.

✦

Names and stories and even dates are important. They remind us of who we are, and they keep us from going missing.

In her unusual volume, *The Woman Warrior: Memoirs of a Girlhood Among Ghosts,* in the section called "Shaman," Maxine Hong Kingston describes a moment in the life of her mother, Brave Orchid, when she has been awakened after a struggle with a ghost. She is afraid that she has gotten lost in that spirit world, and she asks for a familiar ritual to call her back: "'I was afraid, and fear may have driven me out of my body and mind.' Two friends clasped her hands while a third held her head and took each earlobe between thumb and forefinger, wiggling them and chanting, 'Come home, come home, Brave Orchid, who has fought the ghosts and won. Return to To Keung School, Kwangtung City, Kwangtung Province. Your classmates are here waiting for you ... Come home, come home'" (71).

If Cora Mae were here, I would like to wiggle her earlobes and chant softly, "Come back, come back ... return to the Lydia Roper Home, East 40th Street, Norfolk. We are here waiting for you. Cora Mae ... come home." Perhaps it would help her find her way.

So many of the women here need calling back. I hope someone will do that for me.

Names and dates and locations are important. Stories are important.

Chapter Nine

THE HOUSES WE BUILD
THE PLACES WE INHABIT

I KNOW SOME THINGS now about the Lydia Roper Home. I know it was commissioned by Captain John Lonsdale Roper in 1920 and constructed under the direction of Peebles and Ferguson, a local architectural firm. I know that in 1921 the large brick Colonial Revival building was chartered as the Lydia H. Roper Home for the Aged, and intended as a refuge for poor widows. More and more evidence suggests it was Lydia Roper's idea. I know that the Home has operated continuously since 1921, according to its charter, as a home for elderly women. I know that today it provides a home for some of my favorite women. I know that it housed me for eight months in the Winter and Summer and into the Fall of 2013. I know that it continues to call me back.

I know some things about the sacred building of tabernacles and temples and arks in the Hebrew Bible and about the early church in Jerusalem. I know about the churches that Paul established, in the houses of their members, as he traveled to the ends of the known world.

I know that our relationship to those places we inhabit and leave and for which we search is the informing metaphor of the spiritual life in any tradition and is, in fact, the governing reality in our lives. We leave home; the spirit of place is in our bones.

∗◦❀◦∗

Adam and Eve are expelled from the Garden; Abraham is called by Yahweh from his home to a distant promised land; Jacob flees from home after deceiving his father and his brother, but God promises to "bring you back to this land" (Gen. 28:15); in the prophetic book of Jeremiah, God vows to Israel that He will, "gather you from all the nations and all the places where I have driven you ... and I will bring you back to the place from which I sent you into exile" (Jeremiah 29:14); Cain wanders homeless, away from the face of God. David flees his own kingdom as his son pushes to take control. For Jesus, there is no room in the inn, no home but a manger and the road to Jerusalem.

To stake his claim in Norfolk, Virginia, Captain Jack Roper, of Mifflin County, Pennsylvania, built houses.

At age seventeen, I closed the door on the house in the woods and left for college; I closed the door, looked away for only a minute, and home disappeared behind me. By the time I came back for my first weekend, my mother had rented the log house to the people who would eventually buy it, and had moved to Alabama, where her sisters lived. I have spent most of my life looking for home. I have looked in the houses I've owned, in the apartments I've rented, in borrowed rooms, in other people's houses, in churches, in synagogues, in sweat lodges, around every corner. In these old brick buildings in the middle of a city I barely know, no woods anywhere, perhaps I have found it.

It is September; in another month the summer awnings will come down and the windows will be uncovered in my building, letting in the thin winter light. At the end of October, I will have been here for one year. At the Lydia Roper Home, for eight long months, I learned I could be at home anywhere. I came to understand a passage from Esther de Waal's wonderful book, *Seeking God: The Way of St. Benedict*: "Stability means accepting this particular community, this place and these people, this and no other, as the way to God" (57). She is writing here of monastic life, foreign to most of us, but her point is clear. I had to learn to set aside the wish to be somewhere else, and to accept, with Henri Nouwen, that "here and now is what counts and is important" (de Waal, 61). But it was the women in the Bible Study in this particular place, under these particular circumstances, who had to teach me, and they couldn't teach me until I came out of my room. And I did.

The refrain of the classic Crosby, Stills, and Nash song, "Woodstock", written in 1971 at the height of the cultural quest to get back to some mythological state of innocence, is, "We are stardust, we are golden, we are billion year old carbon. And we've got to get ourselves back to the Garden."

In "Gone With the Wind", Scarlet O'Hara, Tara lost to her, cries out in her despair, "I want my mother; I want to go home."

In the archetypal hero's journey, the first step for the hero is to leave home, to go out from his place, to sail like Odysseus or Jason, to aim for the sun like Icarus, to be cast out, like Cain, or called to an unknown place, like Abraham, to be a wanderer of the earth looking always for some promised land.

The final stanza of T. S. Eliot's famous poem, "Four Quartets" begins, "We shall not cease from exploration/And the end of all our exploring/Will be to arrive where we started/And know the place for the first time."

The Episcopal priest writes that "the sacramentality of place is partially because of the way place draws us beyond things."

The Letter to the Hebrews says of those with faith that they "were strangers and foreigners on the earth ... that they are seeking a homeland" (Hebrews 11:13-14).

I know some things about the house John Roper purchased, for himself and his wife, at 314 Freemason Street, a house built in 1854 by James L. Bloodgood, a dry goods merchant originally from Baltimore, a house built in the "Italianate" style, with a center hallway twenty feet wide. I know about the houses Captain Roper built or bought on Freemason Street, one for his son, George, two for his two daughters, and I know a little about the two houses right around the corner on Yarmouth, for his sons, Albert and William. Those houses were side-by-side and "Billy" and Albert shared a garden.

314 Freemason Street

I am learning about Northwood, the summer estate in Blue Ridge Summit, Pennsylvania, where the Ropers spent long vacations. It was on that property that Adele Williams had her studio where she would paint and Ginny Roper would compose her music on the piano that was moved there for her use. I know the two friends sat there companionably for hours and days at a time, month after month, year after year, with easel and keyboard.

The main house at Blue Ridge Summit had six bedrooms and porches all around. Adele's studio was about the size of a small beach cottage, made of native fieldstone, with a fireplace at one end, cathedral ceilings, and a loft. The lawn of the main house spanned five acres. Lydia's great-granddaughter, Molly, says the whole place was "paradise."

Northwood
Blue Ridge Summit, Pennsylvania

I remember the log house my parents built on two hundred acres of woods and streams in the hills of North Georgia. I know that they moved with me in the Winter of 1952 from Atlanta, Georgia, to the tiny town of Cedartown, sixty miles northwest. My father grew up in those hills, and he finally realized his dream of owning land there. They purchased the deep woods and set out to clear a space just large enough to build. With logs from the woods and stones from the creek bank, with no architects or even a blueprint, with the help of two men from the nearby "town" of one general store and a few tarpaper houses, they made a beginning. The wide pine planks for the floors and walls and ceilings had to be brought by train from Alabama. The men were a father and son; the son was blind. He had been a mason for thirty years and he smoothed the mortar and worked in the stones by touch. He made no mistakes. Living in that house was like living inside a beautiful wooden box.

The House on Cedar Creek

My backyard

I know more than I always want to know about the houses
we leave, about the houses we lose, about the houses that
disappear. I know that the Captain and Lydia's son, George,
signed the demolition order for the house at 314 Freemason
Street in 1941, and that sometime in the 1960's the Ropers sold
the property in Pennsylvania. I have seen the documents by
which they turned over the Lydia Roper Home to the Methodist
Church in 1963. I know that many years after the house and
the acres of North Georgia woods had been sold, the log house
burned to the ground. I know that the Jerusalem temple was
destroyed, rebuilt, and destroyed again. There is no temple in
Jerusalem today.

I know about the small white clapboard Episcopal church
where I grew up, and about the exact spots in the woods where my
father found his religion on Sunday mornings when my mother
never failed to try, once again and pointlessly, to convince him
to join us at church in town. I know that my mother took me
to the Episcopal church because she and her sisters and their
brother were born on a dirt farm and grew up in an orphanage
in central Alabama and were determined to leave behind them
forever the dust of that farm and the stench of that orphanage.
The Episcopal Church was one of the emblems of their escape.
Buildings mean something. There is freedom in knowing the
cost of things.

In some ways, the very structure that is the Lydia Roper
Home has made possible all that has happened as we have read
the Bible and tried to attend, as closely as possible, to the Collect
from the Book of Common Prayer, "Blessed Lord, who caused
all holy Scriptures to be written for our learning: Grant us ...
to hear them, read, mark, learn, and inwardly digest them ... "
(236). I think we have done that, and I think we have done it in
part because we have had this old building with its thick stone
walls, its broad porches and back garden, its stairs and hallways,
and its ninety-three years of the memories of women who have
arrived here, lived here, made friendships here, made some kind
of peace here and, inevitably, left here. This house has a story to
tell. Now we are part of that story.

Before David established his kingdom, with its capital and
his palace in Jerusalem, and before Solomon erected the great

Jerusalem temple, God called Moses to "make me a sanctuary, so that I may dwell among them" (Ex. 25:8). The plan for the tabernacle itself is elaborate, and God first orders the people to bring offerings of "gold, silver, bronze; blue, purple, and crimson yarns and fine linen, goats' hair, tanned rams' skins, fine leather, acacia wood, oil for the lamps, spices for the anointing oil and for the fragrant incense, onyx stones and gems to be set in the ephod and for the breast piece" (Ex. 25:3-7).

In this portable tabernacle, God could leave Mt. Sinai and travel with the people. And like Mt. Sinai, it was to have carefully delineated areas of "descending holiness," that would mark how near the people could come to the Divine at the center. Only Moses could sit down with God. Ironically, these limits also served as a necessary protection against God; the tent curtains and the thick veil were a barrier between the Israelites and the sometimes uncontrollable divine power. God often either warned the people to stay at a safe distance or threatened to kill them all. At Mt. Sinai, He cautions Moses, "Do not let either the priests or the people break through to come up to the Lord; otherwise he will break out against them" (Ex. 19:24) (https://bible.org/seriespage/tabernacle-dwelling-place-god-exodus-368-3943).

Robert Frost says, "Before I built a wall I'd ask to know/ What I was walling in or walling out" ("Mending Wall," 1914).

When King David, the man who founded the kingdom of Israel and claimed Jerusalem as its seat, told Yahweh he wanted to build a house fit for Him, David's God said, "No." David established Jerusalem as the center of the life of Israel and, to this day, in psalms and hymns, Jerusalem is called "The City of David." The image of Jerusalem hovers over every Seder, with its promise of "Next year in Jerusalem," and in the Revelation to John, it is a New Jerusalem that is promised to the righteous. David built, and with God's blessing. On the matter of the Temple, God says to his favorite son, "You shall not build a house for my name, for you are a warrior and have shed blood" (1 Chronicles 28:3).

⚜

I spent eight months of 2013 as a resident of the Lydia Roper Home. I know every room, every hallway, every plumbing problem, every furnace crisis; I stood in the community bathroom on the second floor and covered my ears against the shrieking of the alarm during fire drills. I sat in the hallway outside the dining room, waiting for someone to sound the chime. I waited to be handed my medications by the technician on duty; I put my laundry outside my door.

I spent seven of those eight months leading a Bible Study. Week after week, sometimes twice a week, we met and read. I talked about a text that I love; eventually we all talked. We read stories and we told stories; we laughed. One day, Wilma cried. We gathered in the big living room under the portraits of Captain John and Lydia Roper and read the Old Testament three times. We moved to the small parlor, where we are rediscovering the Gospels, the Acts of the Apostles, and Paul's Letters. All this has continued to happen for over a year, in this place that has proved an anchor-hold for us all. The building that John Roper commissioned in 1920 holds us fast. Lydia's Home has become our home.

In the high Middle Ages, an anchor-hold was the small building, often attached to the side of a church, that housed an anchoress, a woman who had chosen to live in solitary withdrawal from the world and in prayer and contemplation. Unlike men, however, who usually withdrew entirely from the secular community and into forest or desert, the anchoress, living near a church, was an important member of her village and a frequent spiritual advisor for its residents (http://www.lordsandladies.org/anchoress.htm).

The *Ancrene Wisse*, or "Anchoresses' Guide," written in the thirteenth century, described the anchor-hold as the place that anchored the anchoress "under a church like an anchor under the side of a ship, to hold it, so that the waves and storms do not pitch it over" (http://d.lib.rochester.edu/teams/text/hasenfratz-ancrene-wisse-introduction).

As we venture further and further into our own lives of contemplation, we have taken to heart Paul's exhortation to the Romans, "Be not conformed to this world, but be ye transformed by the renewing of your mind that ye may prove what is that good, and acceptable, and perfect will of God" (Romans 12:2). We have, all of us, chosen transformation.

Our own anchor-hold is full of women and rich in connections; in this corner of a large old brick building, we are renewed. In this place where we anchor, we have become the load-bearing wall.

There is much that is no longer known about the Lydia Roper Home. I have been told that there are no records, no old brochures, no photographs, no information at all at the Home itself. In Richmond, at the headquarters of the corporation that owns the Lydia Roper Home, they can find nothing about the history of the facility that was given into their care in 1963. I was given a copy of a book, published on the occasion of the corporation's 50th anniversary, in which three pages are devoted to the Lydia Roper Home. I learned that the operational structure of the Home, at the time of its charter, was composed of a "Board of Directresses ... who oversaw daily operations," and a "Board of Trustees, all men," who handled the money (*This Sacred Enterprise* 1999). The other information is available on the Internet.

The researchers at the Slover Library's local history collection recently found this 1946 photograph of an afternoon in the Lydia Roper Home's first-floor living room.

Lydia Roper Home Living Room
23 October 1946

The woman who was a schoolmate of Lydia Roper's great-grandson Al and the administrator at the Lydia Roper Home for nearly twenty years, remembers a stack of old photographs in the drawer of an antique secretary. She describes one in particular, probably from the 1940's, of several residents at a table in the dining room, with members of the kitchen staff, in black uniforms with white aprons, standing behind them. She is also sure there was a small ledger in which notes about daily events were recorded; she remembers that the book was sent to corporate headquarters for safekeeping. The antique secretary is gone, replaced by a modular desk and computer unit. I am told that no one in Richmond knows anything about a ledger.

I have the impression it was a happy house in those days of antique secretaries and daily diaries in which someone recorded every trip to a doctor, every birthday celebration, every small event of the days as they went by. I have heard that the people who lived there and the people who worked there mixed freely, shared personal stories, spent time together. When dining room staff got off early, they watched television with the residents. Doors were open; people visited each other. I think Lydia would have been pleased.

Like nearly everyone connected to the Roper Home, or to the Ropers, Ann Miller heard almost nothing about Lydia Roper. What she did hear, over and over, was that the Lydia Roper Home was Lydia Roper's idea. Like the Roper men and women who guarded this place for four decades, Ann was committed to Lydia's mission to provide a real home for elderly women who needed it. And out from this home, in the earliest days and in the first years of the church's governance, the women went into the world. They went to plays; they went to nearly every play in town. They attended special programs at the Norfolk Zoo and were invited to teas at a local church which hosted a monthly event at which the men served the tea. Any of the women who were fit enough participated in the Senior Olympics, and any who weren't very mobile could toss bean bags around and still get out in the sun and spend an hour or so around new people. Whenever the weather permitted, the residents and staff had cookouts, with burgers and dogs on the grill and plenty of games, in the large back garden, where the Ropers once gathered for Sunday tea.

Irresistibly, every year the Lydia Roper Home sent their senior resident, the woman who had been there the longest, to represent them in the annual "Sweethearts on Parade," sponsored by the city of Norfolk and held at various locations around town. Still happening every Valentine's Day, the event, held in 2014 at the Norfolk Marriott Waterside, is advertised in the *Good Times* magazine with this invitation, "Come see Norfolk's Kings and Queens sachet [sic] down the aisle of the Marriott ballroom in their finest gowns and tuxedos" (Winter 2014, 29).

Lydia Roper's great-granddaughter Bruce sent me the minutes from every meeting of the Board of Directors of the Lydia Roper Home from the first meeting, right after John Roper's death in 1921, through 1963, when the Ropers turned the Home over to the Methodist Church. Those minutes are on microfiche and are currently with my friends at the Slover Library, waiting to be scanned onto a digital file.

"Unless the Lord builds the house, those who build it labor in vain. Unless the Lord watches over the city, the guard watches in vain" (Psalm 167).

Somewhere along the line, the watchmen in charge of the treasures of the Lydia Roper Home were not on guard.

Lydia is gone from the Home that bears her name and with which she was concerned until her death. She endowed the Lydia Roper Home again after John died. Her vision is clear in the charter. I hope the early implementation of that vision will be revealed in those minutes that come from the years when the Board of Directors of the Lydia Roper Home were almost all members of the Roper family.

The history of the houses on Freemason Street and Yarmouth is available through public records and the memories of Lydia's great-grandchildren. There are details missing. It isn't entirely clear whether the double-house was built or purchased by John Roper. The same is true of the Yarmouth houses, where John and Lydia's sons William and Albert lived and shared a garden.

I have no photographs of Adele Williams' studio at Blue Ridge Summit. I don't know exactly when or why that property was sold. I haven't looked very hard for the fate of John Roper's lumber mills. These things hardly seem to matter.

A week ago, I walked down Freemason Street and stopped to look at the double-house. The couple who live there now were working in the yard and we shared stories about the house and the Ropers while Terry took photographs. The houses are a type known as twins, a version of the row house which is still the style of residential architecture by which Lydia Roper's native Philadelphia is known. The Philadelphia twins, like the Ropers' double-house, are mirror images of each other (http://en.wikipedia.org/wiki/Terraced_house#Philadelphia).

The secret of the houses on Freemason Street is that on the second floor a doorway opens between them. Virginia and Margaret must have passed through that doorway many times in the years they lived there. The houses came into Jack Roper's hands, bought or built, somewhere around 1900. Ginny died in 1941; Margaret lived until 1966. I couldn't avoid the hopelessly sentimental thought: Lydia Hand Bowen Roper walked down that street. That street was her home from 1866 until her death in 1930. She came there as a bride; she was ninety years old when she died. All her children except the first, Margaret, were born there. Her infant son, John, died there in 1872. The house that John bought for her is gone, but it was there, one block away from the double-house, another block from her son, George's, home, and just around the corner from William and Albert.

Freemason Street was Lydia Roper's place to inhabit.

☙❦❧

I am still looking for Lydia and I am looking for her in the early life of the Home that bears her name and with which I have been so intimately involved. I have not found the story of Lydia's life at home, with husband and children; I am hoping to find something of her life in the world. I come back to this most important of buildings, the place where I started, the Lydia Roper Home. Her intentions for that Home become clearer as I find more about her other efforts in the city of Norfolk, her work with the poor, the sick and the elderly, with young women just barely surviving their lives alone with children and jobs. It seems to me that Lydia Roper understood the world. The charter for the Roper Home is long and specific. The aphorism "God is in the details" comes to mind. I think Lydia Roper, like so many of her children, was involved with those details.

On a wall on the second floor of the Children's Hospital of the King's Daughters is a row of photographs of past Presidents of the Board. Prominent among them is a picture of Margaret Roper Moss, one of the founders of the King's Daughters in Norfolk and a vital force in the movement that led to the founding of the Children's Hospital, yet another building that houses the dreams and the lives of Roper women. The actual structure that the hospital calls home today is fabulously designed for children. The lobby is a swirl of colors and fabrics on small half-circles of sofas. Bright fish hang from the ceiling, moving in the air of the opened door; a waterfall pours down a wall of glass. Every floor has a different theme. It is a children's paradise. The first children's hospital opened in 1961, five years before Margaret's death, so she saw her dream made concrete; she did not live to see this wonderland it has become. Perhaps these emerging details tell their own story. Perhaps they are a part of Lydia's story.

Margaret Roper Moss
1896-1941

Still, there are stories told by the daughters of the women who knew Margaret, stories about her work at the hospital, stories about her years on the Board of the Roper Home. There are family stories. Caroline remembers being taken by Margaret to one of the baby clinics that the King's Daughters established in Norfolk. Margaret took Molly and Al to the cemetery, where they would clean around the Captain's mausoleum, then spread out a blanket for a picnic lunch. There are stories about Virginia, composing at her piano while Adele Williams painted. There are stories, and more stories, about the sons of John and Lydia Roper. There are no stories about Lydia. But there are these buildings: the house at 314 Freemason Street; the Lydia Roper Home; Margaret's Children's Hospital; Epworth Methodist Church. All those houses where her sons and daughters lived and which surrounded her.

Both the Gospels of Matthew and Luke provide an account of Jesus' birth, but it is only in Luke that we get something approaching a real story, told by a real storyteller. It is Luke's words we have heard over the years in Christmas pageants: "In those days a decree went out from Emperor Augustus that all the world should be registered ... Joseph also went from the town of Nazareth in Galilee to Judea, to the city of David called Bethlehem, because he was descended from the house and family of David. He went to be registered with Mary, to whom he was engaged and who was expecting a child. While they were there, the time came for her to deliver her child. And she gave birth to her firstborn son and wrapped him in bands of cloth, and laid him in a manger, because there was no place for them in the inn" (Luke 2:1-7).

We are brought to life in our stories. We are contained and defined by the places we inhabit: Jesus, by that manger; Moses, by the tabernacle in which his God dwelled; David, by his city and his palace; Solomon, by the temple. John Roper defined himself by building; he built state-of-the-art saw mills, then railroads and canals, then a shipyard; he purchased or constructed large brick houses for himself and all his family. John Lonsdale Roper's last act before his death was to build a home for elderly women, which he named after his wife, Lydia Roper. John Roper was a man of houses. Buildings anchored him to the city of his choice.

There are stories about Jesus, stories about Abraham and Isaac and Jacob, many stories about David. Twenty-one of the twenty-seven books of the New Testament are the Letters written by Paul or his followers, telling Paul's story while they tell the story of the churches Paul founded. The stories of the women in the Bible compel us: the stories of Eve and Sarah and Hagar, of Rebekah and of the sisters, Rachel and Leah, of Naomi and Ruth; the brief glimpses that reveal so much of Mary Magdalene's story.

Stories are important; they move us beyond the facts of our lives.

I type "spirit of place" into the search engine on my laptop and get over three million results. I look at a few. Many are projects or blogs by teams of architects. I think of Frank Lloyd Wright, of course, and then I remember the architect who designed a building in Louisville, Kentucky, when I lived there. His name is Michael Graves and the building he designed, the Humana Tower, is one of the twentieth-century's great landmarks in architecture. Graves has made the statement that any building must balance "pragmatic function and symbolic function." In other words, buildings mean something. The houses we build and the places we inhabit have meaning beyond their use, or even their beauty.

Although God did not allow David to build a house for Him, he set his beloved king the task of gathering all the materials so that his son, Solomon, could build after him. The book of First Chronicles describes David's stockpiling of iron and bronze and cedar. To Solomon he says,

"My son, I had planned to build a house to the name of the Lord my God. But the word of the Lord came to me, saying, 'You have shed much blood and have waged great wars; you shall not build a house to my name ... See, a son shall be born to you; he shall be a man of peace ... he shall build a house for my name" (1 Chronicles 22:7-10).

As when Moses built the tabernacle, Solomon's instructions were explicit, the measurements exact, "These are Solomon's measurements for building the house of God: the length, in cubits of the old standard, was sixty cubits, and the width twenty cubits. The vestibule in front of the nave of the house was twenty cubits long, across the width of the house; and its height was one hundred twenty cubits. He overlaid it inside with pure gold" (2 Chronicles 3:3-4).

On an Internet site called ASK (Associates for Spiritual Knowledge), Ernest L. Martin draws an explicit parallel between the temple and the garden of Eden. The symbolism is unmistakable: the deeper one goes, the closer one gets to the Divine. And in both Garden and temple, there are restrictions that prevent us from becoming "like gods, knowing good and evil."

God is in the details.

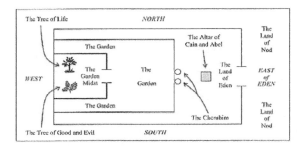

The Garden of Eden
(http://askelm.com/temple/t040301.htm)

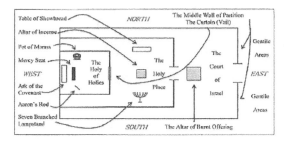

Solomon's Temple in Jerusalem

When Solomon dedicated the temple, "they brought up the ark, the tent of meeting, and all the holy vessels that were in the tent ... sacrificing so many sheep and oxen that they could not be numbered or counted. Then the priests brought the ark of the covenant of the Lord to its place, in the inner sanctuary of the house, in the most holy place, underneath the wings of the cherubim" (2 Chronicles 5: 5-7).

Solomon prayed.

"When Solomon had ended his prayer, fire came down from heaven and consumed the burnt offering and the sacrifices, and the glory of the Lord filled the temple" (2 Chronicles 7:1-6).

"Underneath the wings of the cherubim ... the glory of the Lord filled the temple."

⁂

On the seventh of December, 1930, Lydia Hand Bowen Roper died in her home at 314 Freemason Street in Norfolk, Virginia. She was ninety years old. She had lived in that Italianate mansion for most of her married life. With its twenty foot wide central hallway, its double drawing rooms, its dining room and library, its seven bedrooms and three baths, its sewing room and study, that house had seen the births of Lydia's children and had witnessed the death of her infant son, John. That house, demolished in 1941, was the lodestone of the Roper compound. Until her death, Lydia Roper lived within no more than two blocks of all her grown children. She was contained and defined by the place she inhabited.

I look again at the photograph of the healthy matron of sixty, standing quietly between husband and son; she doesn't look to me like the wife of a wealthy lumber baron, nor like the woman who was mistress of that enormous and elaborate house. She looks like someone else altogether.

Chapter Ten

JUST ANOTHER WEDNESDAY

IT IS WEDNESDAY MORNING, September 3, 2014, and I am looking out these old casement windows, waiting for my ride. Many of the drivers know me and keep a lookout for my cat, Isaac, in the window. The number on my building is hard to read from the street, and they've passed the word along to new drivers, "Look for the white cat in the window." Isaac is at home here.

Isaac

Every May, awnings go up on this building; they, too, are old: striped red and green canvas, more than a little faded. They distinguish us from the 1930's co-ops next door, and they provide welcome shade and cool through the summer months.

On days when the sun is bright and the humidity high, my small living room is like a deep green grotto. I am at home in the pale light; sometimes it is almost chilly.

I'm traveling early these days, arriving at the Lydia Roper Home in time to visit with Nan in her attic room and to sit outside the dining room with the familiar crew—Neal, Lucille, often Kate and, until this week, Evelyn—and with some of the new residents, waiting for the Wednesday breakfast of scrambled eggs, sausage, and a biscuit. It seems a long time since I made the somewhat outrageous claim that, "this is the story of a miracle." Things change, quickly or slowly; not every Wednesday is miraculous.

Today I learn that Evelyn has been in the hospital for nearly a week. Inez barely makes it to the breakfast table because her legs don't support her. When she can no longer walk, she can no longer stay at the Lydia Roper Home. Today Nan is in too much pain to come to Bible Study.

Today was the third Wednesday in a row that three new residents joined us. The faces in our room will change. I don't feel ready for these changes; they seem to be happening very fast and all at once.

Today, for the first time in over a year, the small group that has been there since the first day seemed at risk. Evelyn, in the hospital; Inez, wheeled to breakfast on the seat of her walker. Kate, late because the hairdresser didn't make it on time, missed most of the hour and almost fell asleep the short time she was there. I talked more than I like; I've gotten accustomed to hearing other voices.

I suppose today was one of those inevitable lecture days, as I pulled together the important ideas and people in The Acts of the Apostles and we prepared to move on. The ladies like these quick summaries. Nobody ever takes notes, so a bit of repetition is useful. Sometimes I type up a short recap as a handout. In this case, a lot has happened to interrupt us, and it's easy to forget. We stopped studying Acts for two weeks for Mary Magdalene, then for two more weeks to respond to the questions that guided our own stories. While we were telling those personal stories, we were unmoored from the Scriptures altogether. I am realizing that the connection required of us for the Bible stories is very different than for the stories of our lives. The transition back to the text has proved more difficult than I anticipated.

I don't worry about this temporary loss of momentum. We will be reading Paul's Letter to the Galatians. Paul, it turns out, is a bit of a problem, not quite as straightforward as one might wish for the Apostle to the Gentiles. Paul is difficult; Paul takes up unbending positions, then contradicts himself. Sometimes, he contradicts Jesus. Paul considers himself not only an apostle, though he didn't walk with the Twelve, but in some ways the most important apostle, since the resurrected Jesus spoke to him and gave him a special mission. And Paul is very, very angry with the Galatians. Paul is exactly what we need.

※⁂❋⁂※

In the Lydia Roper Home, our own history speaks to us. Next week we will move back to the large first-floor living room where we started. At breakfast today, Kate asked me if I would consider this move because it will make it easier for Inez to continue to get to Bible Study. Of course that's what we will do; we will keep Inez with us every day that we can.

We will have come full circle.

"And the end of all our exploring/Will be to arrive where we started/ And to know the place for the first time."

Will we know this place differently?

I resist the thought that this symbolic move and the fragility I see in the pioneers mark some kind of ending. I remember what we've just been talking about in Acts. In endings are beginnings. The Ascension marks the end of Jesus' ministry and his life on earth; it marks the beginning of the church. The Crucifixion is the death that is necessary before the Resurrection. Wednesday September 17, 2014, will mark the end of the original Bible Study; it will mark the beginning of a new era in which the pioneers now have the mission of showing the new "church" how it happens.

We are heading toward resurrection.

Again, Jacob comes to mind. Even as he flees from Esau's anger and heads toward his wrestling with God in the night, he is reassured that "I am with you and will keep you wherever you go, and will bring you back to this land; for I will not leave you until I have done what I have promised you" (Gen. 28:15).

In his letter from Jerusalem to the elders among the Babylonian exiles, the prophet Jeremiah brings a message from the Lord, "I will restore your fortunes and gather you from all the nations and all the places where I have driven you ... and I will bring you back to the place from which I sent you into exile" (Jeremiah 29:14).

We are not heading toward resurrection alone.

It will seem strange to be back there. We have made a promise that we will not separate the way we did in the beginning but will find a way to make a smaller space inside that room. We'll figure it out. And there are so many more of us than the original four.

The Acts of the Apostles is about death and resurrection. Jesus has died and has risen. He has ascended into heaven. He is gone. The disciples must have felt completely at a loss about what to do next; they had followed this man for three years, believing him to be the Messiah foretold by the Prophets. He was dead; he returned; he promised to come back again; and he vanished. In the Gospels, the Ascension marks an end: the end to Jesus' ministry. In Luke's theology, it marks the end of the Age of Jesus. In Acts, the Ascension is a beginning; now that Jesus is gone, the Holy Spirit can come to them, as Jesus promised, and the Age of the Church can begin. The body of Christ has departed this world. The church is the new body of Christ. It is not an easy concept.

Acts only briefly describes the death, resurrection, and ascension of Jesus of Nazareth. It tells instead the story of the birth and growing pains of the early church. It changes the rules. The Great Commission has shifted, and the Second Coming has been indefinitely postponed. In Matthew's Gospel, Jesus tells the apostles, "Go nowhere among the Gentiles, and enter no town of the Samaritans" (Matthew 10:5-6). In Acts, their mission is outward, to be "witnesses in Jerusalem, all Judea and Samaria, and to the end of the earth" (Acts 1:8). In two much disputed passages, the Jesus of the Gospels assures his followers that he will return before some of them "taste death" (Luke 9:27) and that "this generation will not pass away" before all he has promised them has come to pass (Matt 24:34). In Acts, when asked when he will return, Jesus responds, "It is not for you to know the times or seasons" (1:6-11).

However we interpret these changes, the tradition of the church on two important issues has been established.

Acts stays focused on its own mission: to tell the story of what happens to The Way, to the followers of Jesus, once Jesus has left them. It is not really a story about Jesus at all. It is a story about the Jerusalem church. It is a story about the beginning of the metamorphosis of the Jesus movement from a Jewish sect to something new, something Gentile. It is the story of Pentecost, a Jewish celebration of the handing down of the Law at Mt. Sinai, and its transformation, at the moment when the Holy Spirit descends on the crowd, to something decidedly not Jewish. It is the story of the Holy Spirit and the powers it bestows on the apostles to preach, to heal, to exorcize—even to raise from the dead.

It is also the story of the two luminaries of Christian tradition: Peter, the rock on which Jesus built his Church, and Paul, the rogue Pharisee and persecutor of Christians, blinded by a light and a voice on the road to Damascus and converted instantly to the most zealous of the apostles.

They provide a useful contrast: Peter, essentially a humble man who, in his shameful cowardice denied Jesus three times but remained staunchly at the head of the persecuted Jerusalem church and Paul, the zealous convert, brazenly confident of his calling by the risen Christ, a man of roads, starting with the road he travelled to Damascus and ending, as Jesus commissioned them all, at "the end of the earth."

Surprisingly, we find similarities. Peter denies Jesus three times, but turns to become the foundation of the church; Paul persecutes Christians, but is transformed into their greatest spokesman. Peter and Paul both understand what it means to make terrible mistakes and to be redeemed by them.

The Conversion of Paul
(Acts 9:1-19a)

Peter Denies Jesus Three Times
(Matthew 26:69-75)

Peter Heals the Lame
Man in the Name of Jesus
(Acts 3:1-2)

Paul the Apostle

What is perhaps the greatest of the differences between them is their experience of Jesus. Paul, in fact, is simply not very interested in Jesus of Nazareth who walked the roads of Galilee, healing and preaching, accompanied by a mixed band of men and women, ultimately ineffective, ultimately executed as a traitor by the Roman Empire. Paul is not very interested at all in the Jesus Peter knew, the Jesus who is touchingly human. In Acts, we see Paul waiting years after his vision near Damascus before going up to Jerusalem to announce himself to the Apostles. We recall that there were no Gospels written at this time; there were, obviously, no Letters from Paul (and those predate the Gospels). Paul had no written stories of the life and ministry of Jesus, the Jewish carpenter from Galilee, and he seems unwilling to spend time with the men who could tell him those stories.

Paul is impatient to be about the business with which the risen Christ has entrusted him—to preach to the Gentiles the gospel of salvation, through the death and—much more importantly—the resurrection of Jesus. Paul preaches the Christ, not the Jewish carpenter.

We have met Paul in Acts—we have done more than meet him. We have gotten to know him as he is seen through the lens of the writer of Luke's Gospel and the Acts of the Apostles. We know his Pharisaic background and learning; we know his passionate hatred of the Jesus sect; we accompanied him on the road to Damascus, where he was traveling to find more Christians to persecute; we witnessed his blinding, his healing by Ananias, his baptism, his announcement of his mission. We have had a thorough introduction to this man, equally zealous in his persecution of the followers of Jesus and in his preaching of the good news of the Messiah to all who would listen.

Neither The Acts of the Apostles nor, of course, Paul's letters, gives any indication of his ultimate fate. Acts leaves him under house arrest in Rome where "He lived two whole years at his own expense and welcomed all who came to him, proclaiming the kingdom of God and teaching about the Lord Jesus Christ with all boldness and without hindrance" (28:31). It is in this section of Acts that Paul makes an early statement of separation from the Jewish community, when he proclaims to those gathered, "Let it be known to you then that this salvation of God has been sent to the Gentiles; they will listen" (28: 30).

We will read what some scholars believe is the first letter Paul wrote, the Epistle to the Galatians. And we will meet Paul unfiltered, not as the subject of a storyteller's skills, but as a man speaking his mind. And Paul is a man who speaks his mind without reserve. In Galatians, we will come face to face with a Paul who is angry and defensive, filled with certainty about his mission, uncertainty about himself, and an unchecked ego. Our first acquaintance with Paul will not be consoling. But nothing in these letters, and nothing in The Acts of the Apostles, suggests that Paul believed his mission to be consolation. He wrote as he believed, with urgency. Paul had only one goal, to which, after his vision, he devoted his life: to preach the good news of salvation through belief in the resurrected Christ. And he preached it with little patience for hesitation or doubt from his listeners.

The New Testament provides the only information we have about Paul, his life and his mission. The narrative in Acts, starting in Chapter 9, focuses on his call, his time in Damascus and his return to Jerusalem, his early preaching of the gospel, and his missionary journeys "to the ends of the earth." Acts provides valuable detail about Paul's career, but this second volume by the writer of Luke's Gospel has a definite message to convey, that of the early and rapid spread of Christianity, and judging by some of Paul's letters it glosses over the rough edges of those first years.

In the eight letters scholars agree were written by him, we come to understand the complexities of Paul's relationships with the churches he establishes and, so, the complexities of the man himself. In our consideration of both Acts and the letters, we will find something that sometimes overshadows both the facts and the theology: Paul's personality.

Although Paul never mentions his place of birth in the letters, the Paul of Acts asserts, "I am a Jew, from Tarsus in Cilicia, a citizen of an important city" (Acts 21:39). Tarsus was a city with a sizable Jewish community. We also learn from Acts that Paul is, by birth, a citizen of Rome. Already we recognize a man of interestingly mixed parts: a Jew, "educated strictly according to our ancestral law, being zealous for God" (22:3), and a man raised as a Roman citizen in the tradition that would have introduced him to the Greek gods and philosophers (Source for all basic information about Paul is Brown, Raymond E. *An Introduction to the New Testament*).

We have to conclude that Paul's life before his vision on the Damascus road was full and pleasant. He had, apparently, the best of both worlds. So we wonder at his decision to leave it behind. Paul explains, in his Letter to Philemon, that he was simply "taken over" by that vision and by his love of Christ (3:12). He was vanquished, and tradition suggests that he moved forward without a backward glance.

By nature, Paul of Tarsus was a zealot. And, whatever happened on the way to Damascus, it changed his direction. From that moment, he believed that God chose "to reveal His Son to me that I might preach him among the Gentiles" (Galatians 1:16).

There is, however, an intriguing and years-long break between Paul's vision and his missionary work. Soon after his conversion and time in Damascus he appears to go to "Arabia"

(Gal. 1:17), which would be nowhere too far from Damascus. He returns to Damascus and also makes a trip to the church of Jerusalem where he visits Peter and James. Then he's in his homeland of Tarsus for quite some time, possibly three or four years. Eventually he heads back to Antioch, and again visits Jerusalem at the time of the famine (probably in the early 40's).

What Paul is doing during these years, we have no way of knowing. Did he spend them in prayer and meditation, preparing himself for his mission? Was he retreating to his home place, with a couple of detours to Jerusalem to be sure his *bona fides* still held with James and Peter? Or did he simply need time to digest what had happened to him? Was he hiding from that call? Did the mysterious ailment, the "thorn" in his flesh, keep him from his journeys? It is hard not to speculate, hard not to wish for the chance to get to know this contradictory and passionate man.

At some point Paul begins his first missionary journey. He made three separate journeys, traveling over most of the known world, spreading the word of salvation through the death and resurrection of Jesus Christ and establishing church communities wherever he could. His letters all arise from those missionary journeys: as he left the new churches, he sent letters back, to praise, to exhort, to admonish. These letters reveal perhaps more than Paul would always have wished.

The Letter to the Galatians begins with Paul's version of the formulaic greeting of the Graeco-Roman letter, with which, of course, he was familiar, "Grace to you and peace from God our Father and the Lord Jesus Christ, who gave himself for our sins to set us free from the present evil age, according to the will of our God and Father, to whom be the glory forever and ever" (1:3-4).

The Galatians, Paul will assert, have strayed from the narrow path of the gospel Paul has preached to them, which is the *unconditional* good news of salvation through Christ's death and resurrection.

He continues, "I am astonished that you are so quickly deserting the one who called you in the grace of Christ and are turning to a different gospel—not that there is another gospel ... But even if ... an angel from heaven should proclaim to you a gospel contrary to what we proclaimed to you, let that one be accursed!" (1:6-9).

The issue is, once again, obedience to the Law of Moses and, especially, that part of the Law that requires circumcision. A group of Jewish Christians, called "Judaizers," who advocate that Gentiles seeking to join the Jesus movement be compelled to observe the Law, have appeared in Galatia since Paul's first visit, insisting that Paul's suspension of that requirement is leaving the new converts without moral guidelines and, so, leading them into sin. In order to become a Christian, according to this group, you must first become a Jew, just as Jesus was a Jew.

The accusation that Paul hurls at the Galatians of listening to "a different gospel," refers to the Judaizers' insistence on justification by works and the need for the church to adhere to many of the rituals and laws of the Hebrew Scriptures. Paul preaches "the superiority of justification by faith and sanctification by the Holy Spirit" (https://bible.org/seriespage/pauline-epistles).

I remind everyone that the Letter is not handed over to be read by the Galatians. It is read aloud by Paul's messenger. It is something meant to be heard, and meant to be heard in the most dramatic way possible. It is a scolding, a warning, and an exhortation. The reading of it must move the listeners to change their ways.

I read the greeting and that first paragraph aloud; I give it all I can muster from a distant background of community theater, "I AM ASTONISHED!"

What does that word "astonished" mean here? Does it just mean he's surprised?

Nan says it's more than just surprised. He's saying he just can't believe what he's heard about them. She thinks he's saying he's disappointed in them, wouldn't have believed they'd do such a thing. She believes he's angry.

And, incidentally, to what is Paul referring with the word "gospel?" Obviously not the Gospels, as yet unwritten. Kate, tentatively, "The good news that was proclaimed when Jesus was born."

Someone else thinks it's beyond that, it's the good news of Jesus' rising and ascending to heaven.

We talk about Paul's loyalties, his belief in the risen Christ, his focus on the Resurrection rather than the Incarnation. Paul's good news is news of salvation through belief in the post-Easter Jesus.

Do we learn anything about Paul himself in this short first passage? What is his tone? Do you get any sense of what he's thinking and feeling? What would it be like to know him?

Kate says immediately, "I'm not sure I'd want to listen to him."

Neal just says he's "full of himself," and I point out that he's also full of Christ and maybe the two things get mixed up sometimes.

Again, I read, pleadingly, furiously, confronting them now:

"Am I now seeking human approval, or God's approval? Or am I trying to please people? If I were still pleasing people, I would not be a servant of Christ ... for I want you to know, brothers and sisters, that the gospel that was proclaimed by me is not of human origin; for I did not receive it from a human source, nor was I taught it, but I received it through a revelation of Jesus Christ" (1:11-12).

Many think that with or without the approval of the Galatians, Paul knows he's right.

We agree that he is concerned about establishing his authority. I suggest there's not a much better way to do that than to claim connection to something supernatural. Visions and revelations are impressive and certainly a part of both Paul's Jewish heritage and the Graeco-Roman world in which he was trained.

Regardless of what we feel, we admit that Paul is "devoted to his beliefs," and it is hard to refute that. Paul is passionately committed to any cause he takes up. Someone says that Paul is most of all committed to Paul, and we do feel his considerable ego investment in this matter of the gospel he brings. We're just not sure that's a bad thing; does it take a certain amount of ego to do what Paul has set out to do? Didn't they all need it, all those ranting prophets? Heaven knows King David was filled with his ambition to be acceptable before God, if only his appetites hadn't interfered. But God liked it, and God loved David. I once heard Yahweh described as "the God who fell in love with a king."

Kate wants to know what it does for us today. When I ask what "what" does for us today, she says, "Oh, all of it."

We somehow start talking about the conflict between a belief in science and our belief in God: the centuries-old argument between science and religion. That argument doesn't burn quite so universally hot today as lines are crossed and physicists start looking for something they call the "God Particle." It still surfaces, however, in much of Christianity's struggle between the body and the spirit, between our animal nature and our souls- starting with Paul's controversial injunctions against sexuality. Much has been written about Paul's opinions on sexuality. Recently I read that, in fact, Paul possibly does not take an absolute stand against sex but, because he believes the world is about to end, opposes everything that might distract from pure devotion to Christ as the only path to salvation. It makes a certain amount of sense, although there are those shrill passages about sexuality.

We choose not to wade further today into the morass of Paul's views on sex, and we are rescued by a question that leads down a slightly different path. "What about this circumcision?"

After the expected laughter and the comment from someone that this is a big deal and not peanuts (or, as another of my senior citizens notes, "Not a peanut!"), the group, by now, is reduced to near hysterics. I think Neal is actually snorting.

I try to respond seriously. It is all about this idea, central to Judaism, of a "covenant in the flesh" between Yahweh and his people, Israel. It comes before everything else. And, in that way of the Hebrew Bible, it absolutely denies the separation of body and soul. Here is the ultimate spiritual commitment, sealed with the letting of blood and the offer of flesh.

I ask the question of these women, gathered here, many of whom spent a full year together steeped in these Israelite traditions and rituals: what group of people is automatically denied access to the community by this covenant? Surprisingly, it takes them a long time to see it. The ritual of circumcision excludes women.

I talk briefly about the idea that came to me during my very first year of teaching the Bible, that in fact Yahweh does have a covenant in the flesh with these women we have come to know so well. In story after story, the wives of Israel are barren. Yahweh promises them children and, as with Sarah, "The Lord dealt with Sarah as he had said, and the Lord did for Sarah as he had promised. Sarah conceived ... " The list of Israel's barren wives is long: Sarah, Rebekah, Rachel, Leah. Even with young Mary, a virgin, the angel tells her that "The Holy Spirit will come upon you, and the power of the Most High will overshadow you." And in every case, these women whose stories tell us they are doing God's work in whatever unorthodox ways, conceive and bear sons for God's chosen people. A covenant in the flesh; a covenant with the wombs of Israel.

The messenger speaks more quietly; the beginning of this part of Paul's letter is confiding, confessional. He wants them to know he is vulnerable, trusting, wholly theirs if only they will come back to the gospel he preaches. "You have heard, no doubt, of my earlier life in Judaism. I was violently persecuting the church of God and was trying to destroy it. I advanced in Judaism beyond many among my people of the same age, for I was far more zealous for the traditions of my ancestors. But when God, who had set me apart before I was born and called me through his grace, was pleased to reveal his Son to me, so that I might proclaim him among the Gentiles, I did not confer with any human being, nor did I go up to Jerusalem to those who were already apostles before me ... " (1:13-17).

We will need to look closely at this man, this Apostle to the Gentiles, called by the Christ himself, given the mantle of suffering to bear for his Lord, chosen in spite of his sins. One thing this early letter reveals is Paul's native cleverness: he moves easily from one mood to the next: scolding, confiding, pleading, and exhorting, and it all seems to work. He is a master of the rhetorical skills of the Greco-Roman world in which he grew up. I believe he would have chosen his messenger carefully, a man whose oratorical abilities would communicate the subtleties of both Paul's message and his personality. It was, in all likelihood, the absence of that personality in their midst that made the Galatians susceptible to the new preachers of the gospel.

Why has Paul changed his tone here? Why is he reminding the Galatians of his past sins against the church?

And what is his intention in telling them again that he was called by God, through Christ, and didn't "go up to Jerusalem"?

Is he just bragging? Is it more complicated than that? Paul is interesting; Paul is not simple. The teacher in me is chewing on this one.

We have run out of time and will begin with these questions next week.

Today, we have met on the front porch; the weather is a little cool, what a friend calls "jacket weather." We linger. We talk more about the covenant in the flesh; we talk about Paul with his odd mix of Jew and Greek. Kate and I remember when she asked whether Luke was really a physician. Part of the evidence which suggests that Luke, who perhaps traveled with Paul, was a man of medicine, are the references to Paul's mysterious ailments, his "thorn in the flesh" (2 Cor. 12:7). Since we are reading Galatians, I remind everyone that it is in this letter that Paul refers several times to possible physical problems. He writes about "my trial which was in the flesh" (4:13) and claims to "bear in my body the marks of the Lord Jesus" (6:17).

We have something else to consider about this man: his health might not have been good. He might have been in pain. We do know that he was beaten on several occasions as he preached his gospel. There was a shipwreck. Not an easy life after that vision of the Christ. Paul suffered, as Ananias predicted.

There has always been a theory about Paul's health as it relates to the experience on the road to Damascus. Articles in medical journals over the years periodically revive the idea that Paul was an epileptic, and that the vision of bright light, the auditory hallucinations, and the temporary blindness were symptomatic of a *grand mal* seizure.

Next week we will return to our search for Paul who is, in many ways, as elusive as Lydia Roper.

This Wednesday isn't a successful one. I don't know if I was just "off," or if Paul's ideas in Galatians are really too complicated and confusing to allow for ready comprehension, let alone discussion. Lots of head-shaking today; lots of the ladies getting up and down, restless, going in and out of the living room. I started, as I usually do, with a quick summary of what we talked about last week: that Paul's frequent references to "scripture" refer to the Hebrew Bible, almost certainly the Septuagint, the Greek translation completed sometime between 300-200 BCE.

It is somehow difficult for people to grasp that Paul didn't have the Gospels and that when he refers to the "gospel," he is talking only about the message, which he delivers, of salvation through belief in the risen Christ.

We talked about Paul's increasing rejection of the Law of Moses. That Law was more than the obvious stumbling block of circumcision; it contained the Ten Commandments, elaborate dietary laws, and hundreds of laws governing every aspect of life in the community and relations with others. In the beginning of his life as Apostle to the Gentiles, Paul believed that the Law was unnecessary for justification; later, he writes that it is actually an impediment to salvation through faith (Gal. 5:1-6). Newly minted Christians must choose between the religion of the ancient Israelites and the new church. They must choose between the Law and faith.

We also talked last week about Paul's vision on the road to Damascus, his blindness, and his instant conversion from zealous persecutor of Christians to zealous preacher of the gospel of Christ. We talked about Paul's dramatic, sometimes contradictory, personality.

As I wrestle with Paul's ideas, I understand his imperative that we "pray without ceasing." I haven't seen this many glazed looks since the first time I tried to introduce Faulkner to high school juniors.

Paul's messenger continues his narrative: "But when Cephas [Peter] came to Antioch, I opposed him to his face, because he stood self-condemned; for until certain people came from James, he used to eat with the Gentiles. But after they came, he drew back and kept himself separate for fear of the circumcision faction ... I said to Cephas, before them all, 'If you, though a Jew, live like a Gentile and not like a Jew, how can you compel the Gentiles to live like Jews?' " (2:11-14).

Paul insults and accuses Peter "to his face", and I ask why this is such an outrageous thing to do. Who is this "Cephas," or Peter, that he should be untouchable? Several of the ladies nod and say "the Rock on which I build my church." In Matthew's Gospel, written long after this Letter to the Galatians, Jesus says to Peter, "You are Peter, and on this rock I will build my church, and the gates of Hades will not prevail against it. I will give you the keys of the kingdom and whatever you bind on earth will be bound in heaven, and whatever you loose on earth will be loosed in heaven" (Matt. 17-19).

Paul accuses Peter of hypocrisy, of eating freely with Gentiles until James sends a delegation from Jerusalem to check on him. Paul accuses Peter of "not acting consistently with the truth of the gospel," and the only gospel Paul acknowledges is the gospel he preaches. It is clear in his letter that the Galatians have questioned not only the means of salvation but Paul's authority to preach the gospel of Jesus against the greater authority of the Jerusalem Apostles who had known Jesus. Paul is defending the Pauline gospel and himself personally.

Every piece of the puzzle that is Paul points to the ego that pushes him away from the apostles, the Jerusalem church, and Jewish Christians, and toward a new entity of largely Gentile churches established by Paul and his followers and spread across the Roman Empire.

I have talked too much; we are all tired. I go home to think through what will happen next. This is only the first of Paul's letters; even with our edited line-up, we still have five to go. In order to gather my own thoughts, I type an extra handout; I call it "Paul: What We Know So Far." I find that we actually know a good deal.

⁂

It is Wednesday October 22. We come together in the living room, with its wide-screen television and its portraits of Captain John and Lydia Roper. As usual, I have to turn off the television. We hardly ever notice the portraits.

Before reading the extra handouts, we look at the last passage from Galatians, in which Paul claims, among other things, that "the scripture has imprisoned all things under the power of sin," and that "the law was our disciplinarian until Christ came, so that we might be justified by faith." I am reminded of the *felix culpa*, the fortunate fall, in which suffering was introduced into the world so that we would need Jesus to redeem us. If Adam and Eve had not disobeyed, we wouldn't have Jesus; if the Law hadn't forced us into sin, we wouldn't need Christ. I am reminded of the questions about the blind man Jesus heals: was he blind because he sinned? Was he blind because his parents sinned? No, he was blind so that God could show his power.

Finally, in a long passage from Chapter Five of Galatians, Paul makes his most complete break with the Law by claiming not that it is unnecessary, and not that it doesn't matter, but that "if you let yourselves be circumcised, Christ will be of no benefit to you." Then he turns right around to soften the blow with, "For in Christ Jesus neither circumcision nor uncircumcision counts for anything; the only thing that counts is faith working through love." Can we possibly figure this man out?

My first question is large. Do you believe we are justified, or saved, by good works, by being good people, or by faith in the saving power of the crucified and resurrected Christ?

The response is nearly unanimous. We are justified by faith. Christianity today is, for the most part, Pauline Christianity.

And I play the Devil's Advocate. What about a serial killer, unrepentant, who has faith in Jesus? Some say there's always hope; others, that some things are unforgivable. I'm not sure we've made much progress, but I stand by my belief that the questions are the important thing, perhaps the only thing. I don't know about answers.

I do know about summaries, though, and now I hand around my sheet on Paul as we have come to know him in just these two books, the Acts of the Apostles and the Letter to the Galatians. I have made short lists of specific details of Paul's life and his beliefs. I have included a section about Paul's personality, which requires a bit more speculation but, in one case at least, Paul himself tells us that he is, "zealous for the traditions of my ancestors." I think we are on safe ground to say that Paul is zealous for anything he undertakes; he is as committed to persecuting Christians as he is to preaching the good news of Christ. We can say that he is a proud man, refusing human counsel after his vision of the risen Christ, going to Jerusalem briefly, then not again for fourteen years. We can conclude that he is not well, that he suffers from some kind of chronic pain or "ailment." We know about his missionary journeys from Acts. We know from Galatians that the cornerstone of his theology is that we are justified by faith in Christ, and by nothing else.

We seem, in a way, to have moved forward very little in these pages; we started with Luke's Gospel and are concluding with one of Paul's earliest letters, and so one of the oldest documents in the New Testament. We have so far to go: in our study of the Bible, in our forging of relationships, in our search for Paul and for Lydia and for God, in our discovery of ourselves. The calendars I've made get us through Paul's Letters to the Thessalonians, the Philippians, the churches at Corinth and Rome. They pull us into Hebrews, a letter not written by Paul but one of the most beautiful pieces of prose in the Bible. We will talk about First Corinthians for the last time on New Year's Eve. We will read the Letter to the Romans by early February of 2015. We will complete Hebrews in mid-March. In early April we will begin John's Gospel. In May or early June, we will embark on our journey into the Revelation to John. I don't believe we will be through with Revelation before July. Catherine warned me, before she left, that Revelation would take about three times longer than whatever I estimated.

We have much left to do. We have accomplished wonders already. We have grown from our small group of silent pioneers to this exuberant dozen, changing and growing every day, making outrageous demands on ourselves, on each other, on the Scriptures, and on God. We are holding on and refusing to let go. I, for one, have been both wounded and blessed by these encounters. I will come back every week for as long as I can make it up those stairs.

I cannot imagine my life without this place, this work, and these women. I almost cannot believe that I have come to where I am from who and where I was on the day I walked up those stairs for the first time. I recall the words of the old hymn, "I once was lost, but now I'm found." Is there possibly a better description than "amazing grace" for what has befallen us here? We are found, indeed.

Today, Evelyn came back to Bible Study. Her eyes were bright; she could hear me; she smiled all the way through the hour. Today, Kate arrived a little late and fell asleep. Today Inez is still in rehab, and I don't know when I'll be able to get back out to see her. Wilma is gone; Cora Mae is gone. We have no idea where they are. They went through the door and disappeared; we have no way to find them. They, too, are on some list of former residents and friends whose whereabouts we cannot know.

Today, we completed our study of Paul's Letter to the "foolish Galatians." In two weeks, we will begin to read Thessalonians, a letter much different in tone, showing us a kinder, gentler Paul. We will continue.

Epilogue

"There's some questions got answers and some haven't."

MR. WHITEHEAD, THE GARDENER in Peter Weir's 1975 film, *Picnic at Hanging Rock,* offers this piece of homespun wisdom when all investigation, and much speculation, has failed to turn up any clues to the disappearance of a teacher and five schoolgirls on an outing in the Outback. The film is based on a true story.

I have three photographs: one of a young Lydia, how young it isn't possible to tell; one of Lydia, with the Captain, their thirty-year-old son, William, and William's baby daughter, Elizabeth, in which Lydia is sixty; and a picture taken when she was probably in her eighties.

I have wanted to know her, have been obsessed with knowing what she wanted and what she found in the Tidewater region of Virginia, this land where the water level rises and falls with the pull of the moon and flooding is frequent. Some say that Tidewater Virginia is a state of mind. Others have survey maps that mark out the exact boundaries of this country of water.

Lydia spent over sixty years of her life here. What dream was she chasing? Perhaps it is enough to believe that she was chasing one, that she wanted something badly enough to leave home and family, to travel to a southern city the year the Civil War ended, to cast her lot with a carpetbagger who had his own dream. John Roper must have been busy with his sawmills and his plans for an empire. Empire building takes time.

Maybe Lydia Roper is a question that doesn't have an answer. Or maybe what Molly says is true: "You have found Lydia; you have found her in Albert; you have found her in me."

I have found Molly and Al, an undisputed miracle. I want to find Lydia in herself. I want to see what she saw and know what she knew. Lydia was ninety years old when she died. It was a long life, long and full and rich: with a husband; with five children; with days full of work in the hospitals and shelters of Norfolk, Virginia. A beautiful building dedicated to the care of poor, elderly women was named for her; I found two sources that claim a schooner was named for her, sometime in the 1870's or '80's. The building is a place where life winds down; the ship, perhaps loaded with lumber from her husband's mills, was always looking forward, into the next adventure. I like to believe that the women at the Lydia Roper Home are headed toward their next adventure. Perhaps, like Jesus, they have set their faces toward Jerusalem.

I wonder why thinking about her makes me sad, although certainly not as sad with these photographs in hand—in her teens, at sixty, near eighty; not as sad having seen the album her daughter edited one summer in New Jersey; more nearly content having heard the stories of her grown children and her grandchildren; even happy, now that I have experienced the kindness of her great-grandchildren, now that I have seen that picture of her husband beside her, still handsome, without the full beard of his later years. Most days, hardly sad at all.

I am intemperate. I want Lydia in every decade.

Where is the Lydia of the child-bearing years, the Lydia who gave birth to six children in the thirteen years between 1866 and 1879, in the years between her twenty-sixth and her thirty-ninth birthdays? Where is Lydia, still in her thirties, shepherding four small children and Albert, the youngest, a babe in arms, on the short walk to Granby Street Methodist Church? Where is the forty-year-old Lydia, Albert not quite two, Margaret now fourteen? Where is Lydia in her fifties, Albert just approaching adolescence, Margaret twenty-four, having been at her work with the King's Daughters for nearly five years? Lydia, by then, must have been out on the streets of Norfolk herself, hand on the foreheads of patients at the hospital, listening to the problems of young women with jobs, perhaps children, and taking action to solve those problems with more than shelters.

Where is the Lydia who planned that beach retreat?

Her first child was born as soon as possible after she married and came south. There wasn't much time to take a breath, but that was not unusual for the time. Even with the photographs, with the dates of all the important life events, with information about her charitable work and her Sunday school classes. Even knowing she was loved and remembered in Norfolk, there is still not one single story. There is no buggy-whipper, no Ginny and Adele in the studio, no album of a summer at Ocean Grove, no Roper, North Carolina, no silent partner Baird, no father's death, mother's struggle, not one story. We know nothing but statistics about her parents, either. No stories. Not one family reminiscence.

I have pictures now; Lydia Roper has a face. I know she was neither beautiful nor stylish as a young girl. I know she had a tall, dark-haired son whose shoulder she touched as they posed for a photograph. I know that her nose was too large and her gaze unwavering. I know that Captain John Lonsdale Roper once looked like a man with whom a girl from Philadelphia might fall in love. I know that the family in the decades after Lydia's death had Sunday teas in the garden at the Lydia Roper Home. I know that her oldest child, Margaret, is remembered by this generation of Ropers.

Molly says that if there is even one comparison made between her life and the life of her "Tante Margaret" she "will die a happy woman." She says that Margaret, already an old woman when Molly was a child, taught her that unconditional love exists.

Am I only to know Lydia by what she left behind? By what she did? By what her children did? By what I want to know? By what I imagine? Is it possible those are the only ways we ever know anyone?

I don't quite believe it. I am not ready to give up. I am not ready to give up looking for Lydia because I want to know what Lydia was looking for.

I am not ready to give up.

Some questions have increasingly complex answers: I learn on Labor Day that Kate, in addition to singing, is an accomplished bell ringer. On Wednesday morning at breakfast, I will ask her for some stories.

And on Labor Day I learn that Cora Mae has left the Lydia Roper Home. I can get no information about where she has gone, or why. There are still a few things in her room, but she is not there. I've been afraid this was happening. But there was no notice, no chance to say goodbye. People vanish; friends vanish.

Catherine went back to the assisted living facility where she lived before she came to the Roper Home. The week she moved, she gave me her new address and phone number. I sent a card to be there when she arrived.

There is no chance of that with Cora Mae. I would love to call her son, as I called Kate's, to tell him how much I enjoyed his mother, that she had begun to show up for Bible Study. I don't think that's going to happen.

I remember every time I saw her, slipping around doorways, a little person, self-contained, with that fairy mind, scattered, flying apart in all directions. I remember the day Cora Mae spoke up, loud and clear, "Now I think I belong here; it's all right for me to come."

I remember that she wandered out the door and was gone all one day. Now she has wandered out again, and this time we will not find her.

On the day that I am writing this I talk to Evelyn's daughter, Carolyn, and learn that Evelyn was in the hospital for a week and has now gone to a rehab center very near the Roper Home. Tomorrow I will visit both her and Catherine. Whatever happens, they are gone from that immediate circle of the Bible Study. Their chairs are taken by new women.

Terry and I set aside Sunday morning for visits. We head out to neighboring Chesapeake to find Catherine's new home. It is a one-story modern building, with well-maintained grounds and a lobby that looks like a moderately expensive motel; it is no different than most of the better assisted living and nursing facilities I have seen over the years. Catherine's room is large and nicely arranged; she tells me that one of our favorite housekeepers came from Lydia Roper on her day off and unpacked all her boxes. Everything in Catherine's room is put away, and she is pleased, although she claims not to know where anything is.

We are ready to leave just at lunchtime, and we walk slowly to keep Catherine company down the long hall. We leave her at the door to a large and welcoming dining room. She assures us that the food is delicious, just like home-cooked.

We arrive at Evelyn's rehab center just as the technician comes in for some tests, so we head back to the lobby to wait. Evelyn is adjusting. She is there to learn to walk again so she can get back to the Lydia Roper Home, and she is very focused and determined. I know she is tired.

As always, Evelyn is trying hard to be cheerful. She has clearly worked most of her life to put the best face she can on sometimes difficult circumstances. Today the veneer is in danger of cracking. She cries from the fear of never walking again and from the sheer outrage of her failing eyesight. She is very glad to see us, and she talks in some detail about the physical therapy she has three times a day. She had this same condition several years ago and was in rehab for six weeks, so I understand we can't expect anything to improve right away. Before we leave, Evelyn is sitting up straighter. She is going to fight, and she is going to pray. I resist surrendering to my own fear that she won't make it back at all.

The losses and the changes pile up. The dynamics of the Bible Study will shift as the pioneers leave and new women arrive. I should be accustomed to a yearly leave-taking from the decades teaching high school students. Every June, all the seniors left to start their lives. Every June, it was painful. Every Fall, we started new.

The Wednesday Bible Study at the Lydia Roper Home will be going on for a very long time, indeed; by my calculations, we won't get through the New Testament before June or July of 2015. Already the new ladies, and some of the old, are asking if I'll go through the Old Testament again.

I haven't lost Lydia Roper; I have simply never quite found her. I am not ready to give up.

When I first started writing, the Baptist preacher suggested that I call this story about a group of women studying the Bible, "Looking for Lydia." I thought he was joking. Now that seems the only possible title.

I have looked for Lydia Roper, and I have found vital statistics from census records and from a card at the cemetery; information about her public charitable work from several obituaries, and three photographs, sent to me by family members. I have spoken at length with her great-grandchildren whose responses I have recorded. The very first thing that Albert Roper said in answer to my question about her was, "Nobody ever talked about her." I remember he seemed puzzled by the question. Bruce Forsberg says that three generations of her family, all on the Board at the Roper Home, never heard a personal word about Lydia Roper.

I know when she was born, and when she died. I know when and where she was married. I know when her children were born; I know when the infant John was born and when he died. I even know when Lydia's parents were born and when they died. I don't know what her father, David Bowen, did for a living because the only clue I have is an old tax record, and the handwriting in the column for *Occupation* is illegible. I believe the names of her siblings are available on ancestry.com. I saw them, but didn't feel it necessary to write them down. I suppose I can go back. I have found a great deal. I do not feel I have found Lydia.

Why am I not satisfied? What did I want?

I wanted a fully-fledged Lydia, with family stories and stacks of photographs. I wanted Lydia during the twenty-five Philadelphia years; I would have liked knowing where she lived, what her house was like. I wanted photographs with her young husband. I wanted the years between sixty and ninety. Was she a good grandmother? Did she spend time with George's children, with William's and Albert's? Did she get down on the floor to play with Jack and Isobel, and later with Elizabeth and Leighton and Margaret? Did she bake cookies for them? Did they spend the night in her huge house? I wanted to know what women's shelters she built, wanted stories and photographs of her on the sidewalks, at least one photograph of her sharing a laugh with some of the women she brought to those shelters. I wanted everything. I wanted stories.

And, even as I type the words, I realize that there *are* stories; there are stories I heard very early, stories I investigated and dismissed. There are stories that brought me no closer to Lydia Roper, stories that, in fact, seemed to widen the distance. But there *are* stories about Lydia.

To begin, there is the story about Lydia's age. It is a persistent story, never quite disappearing. This story insists that Lydia Bowen was half the age of her husband, that she was fifteen years old when she married the thirty-year-old Jack Roper. This is the story that would explain the idea that the photograph of the schoolgirl, Lydia, is a photograph of Lydia, the new bride. Every public record lists Lydia's age, at the time of her marriage, as twenty-five to John's thirty years. Lydia's birthdate, in every census and on her interment card at Elmwood Cemetery, is September 8, 1840. The story claims that some records indicate Lydia was born in 1850. I have found no such records. One look at that early photograph by a woman whose credentials make her a "costume historian," confirms that the hair and the clothing are those of a very young girl in the nineteenth century. They are not the hair and clothing of a young girl just married or even about to be married. The photograph of Lydia with the Captain and their son William, taken in 1900, tells anyone that Lydia Roper was not fifteen years younger than her husband. Still, there is the story; the story continues to be told.

There is also the story of Lydia Bowen, Quaker. It's a good story. Lydia, raised by her Quaker parents, in the solid tradition and large community of Philadelphia Friends, was to marry John Roper, perhaps a Methodist, perhaps not of any affiliation, from Mifflin County. The story goes that, on the way to Norfolk after the wedding, Captain Roper advised his Quaker bride that they were going to be Methodists. In spite of her enforced conversion, however, Lydia never lost her Quaker ways; she was known for her spiritual disciplines of solitude and prayer. A very good story. I spent the better part of a week, and monopolized hours of what I feel sure was the already crowded schedule of the Curator of Quaker Collections at Haverford College, searching their database for the Hands and the Bowens. Haverford College houses the Quaker records for Philadelphia, just as Bryn Mawr holds them for New York City. No Hands or Bowens appear in those Philadelphia records. There is no evidence that Lydia was a Quaker or that either her parents or her grandparents were Quakers. Still, it makes a grand story.

There are more, of course. There is the still undocumented claim that somewhere is an official statement that the Lydia Roper Home was dedicated to the care of "widows of Confederate soldiers." I read this in several places; it was always in quotation marks, never with a citation. I first read it in an online advertisement for a book published locally in 2006 called *Colonial Place and Riverview: One-Hundred Years of History,* by Artemis Stoll and Susan Van Hecke. I spoke with Ms. Stoll and she told me frankly that she had no idea where the quote came from. She referred me to several local historians who were eager to help, sent me all sorts of historical materials from the Internet, answered my questions promptly and courteously, seemed genuinely interested, but didn't know the source of that particular description or the original purpose of the Lydia Roper Home.

But it does make for what might be my favorite story: the Union soldier, driven by ambition, product of a hardscrabble youth with a single mother struggling to make ends meet, serves in the Army during the Civil War, is stationed in the Norfolk area, spots the timber, and from his days in the cutthroat California gold mines, understands the way things work, convinces a friend to join him, and sets out to make his fortune and his name cutting timber and shipping lumber out of the South. Years later, a wealthy old man, he has a final awakening, repents and, one month before his death, makes his amends to the Confederacy in the person of its impoverished widows. In other words, Captain Jack Roper, of the Pennsylvania Eleventh Division of the Army of the United States of America, saw what he wanted, saw what he could get, and came back and got it. With him, he brought his Philadelphia bride. He made his fortune, settled his family, and created himself as one of the city's most well-known philanthropists.

From the backwoods of Pennsylvania to the California gold rush; from the Union Army to the post-Civil War South; from the rough mining camps of the newly burgeoning lumber industry to the Board rooms and charitable institutions of his adopted city, Captain Jack Roper made his own story come true.

There seems to be no way to either verify or refute the story that Jack Roper dedicated the Lydia H. Roper Home to the support of poor Confederate widows; there is actually no evidence to verify that the Lydia H. Roper Home was even his idea.

In the absence of evidence, the stories persist. Captain Roper is something of a legend in Tidewater Virginia, even today.

The last of the stories about Lydia Roper is the mystery of the two little girls who died. This story says that Lydia Roper gave birth to not six but eight children between 1866 and 1879. The two children left out of the records are Mollie S. Roper, suspected of dying young of unspecified causes, and a baby, Lydia Roper, who died early of "failure to thrive." Nothing else is known or said about these babies. The story comes from a member of Lydia's family; no one else in the family has heard it.

Molly, in her usual considering way, just said, "Well, maybe; I don't know why not."

Still, in spite of all the stories, true and probably not, I have found not one that gives me Lydia in the way I want. I know many more things *about* her than I ever expected, but I don't have any stories to give me a sense of who she was, what impact she had on a room when she entered it, what made her cry, what made her laugh, who she loved. I think perhaps the most poignant moment in this search for Lydia Roper was when I saw that census report that listed her as "Liddy Roper." It was a brief glimpse of someone I might have known. I saw her turning the corner. I want to call her back.

The temptation is great to continue adding to the Epilogue, snatching it from the hands even of a publisher to tack on just one more update. In the few days just past, I have found Inez, who is in a room next door to Evelyn at the rehab center. Today, Terry and I climbed in the car again, right after Bible Study, to make the rounds. We took copies of all the Bible Study handouts to Catherine, who requested them on our last visit; we sat with Evelyn, who is going tomorrow, with her daughter and a physical therapist, for a trial run back to the Roper Home. The therapist will put Evelyn through her paces, testing to see how much she might be able to do on her own. She's nervous that she won't do well, and won't be able, as she said today, "to go home." We waited for Inez to complete her therapy, then Terry got a few great-looking photographs. We are all smiling; it was good to be together again.

I remember two pieces of wisdom, shared over the years by two friends from Michigan. The first is, simply, that if we are seeking God we have already found God. The second, "If I beat a path to God, God will come to me on the path that I have beaten."

I have beaten my path to Lydia Hand Bowen Roper. Will she come to me on it one day?

Just yesterday I placed in my DVD player a disc labeled "Roper Home Movies." Several years ago, Molly took all the family home movies, clearly the product of a camera that used reel-to-reel film, and had them transferred to this disc. The entire hour has that jerky, amusing, slightly surreal quality of an old silent film, and whoever did the work has added a soundtrack of music from the 20's and 30's. It begins with the family on their property at Blue Ridge Summit; everyone is there. I can't identify anyone, of course, but tomorrow Al is coming over to watch it with me and put the now-familiar names to the faces on this film. For those he can't recall, I will have the chance to watch it again with Molly when I head to Lynchburg for the weekend, to meet this new friend in person.

There are fifteen minutes or more of a very old woman, obviously someone important, who is celebrating her birthday, sometime in September. Lydia Roper would have been eighty-eight in 1928, when these segments are dated. She was born in September. The old woman on the film has a very large nose. I try not to get my hopes up.

Somewhere close to the end of the film, the scene changes. We are now in the back garden of the Lydia Roper Home in 1937; the residents come trooping out, gloves on, croquet mallets in hand, to tend their flower garden, to play croquet on the lawn, and to sit down to tea with some of the members of the Roper family. People are smiling; a few are laughing.

I will take that DVD to the Lydia Roper Home one Wednesday soon and I will show the Bible ladies all the footage of this place where they live. Many of them were young women in 1937.

Kate was born in 1916. In 1937, she was twenty-one.

Nan was a teenager; Catherine was in her early twenties.

Inez graduated from high school in 1941.

Evelyn was twenty, already married.

We will watch the film of the Lydia Roper Home together.

The preacher told me that, "Looking for Lydia is like looking for God, and you're doing both. We are all looking for Lydia. We are all looking for that something we may or may not find, but the search for which defines our lives. In the course of that search we find frustration, disappointment, loss, and grief, but we also find much that we didn't expect—work and love and relationships and joy."

And so, the ladies at the Roper Home and I are looking for God and Lydia and possibly ourselves. We have sometimes been frustrated, sometimes afraid; we have found good work, we have found each other. We are discovering God in some new ways.

For me, it's a bargain.

Thoughts After the Last Curtain

WHERE WE GO FROM HERE

From here, we go to Philadelphia.

Early in my efforts to discover Lydia Roper's story, I included a cursory search into her life in Philadelphia before she met and married John Lonsdale Roper. Lydia Hand Bowen was twenty-five years old on the day of her small wedding, a spinster by the standards of nineteenth-century Philadelphia. What was she doing? Of what ordinary details did her life consist? Was she, as one of her great-granddaughters heard, active in the Underground Railroad, ferrying runaway slaves to freedom? Did she simply stay at home, sew, and read novels? In what part of the city did she live? Is that neighborhood still standing? What kind of neighborhood was it between 1840 and 1865? What was her father's profession? Did her family attend church?

I wasn't able to find answers to any of those questions.

Once I realized I had my work cut out for me in Norfolk, I put Philadelphia on hold.

Lydia's life in Norfolk from 1866 until her death in 1930 was difficult enough to trace; for a long time, I could find almost nothing. Even later, it has been slow going and there remain more questions than answers. I still have found not one photograph of her between the ages of fifteen and sixty. And, of course, no stories.

Having exhausted, at least for the time being, the resources for researching the life of Lydia Roper during her sixty years in Norfolk, Virginia, I turn my attention back to the lost twenty-five years in the life of Lydia Hand Bowen of Philadelphia. This period interested me from the beginning since I soon grew fascinated by Lydia herself, and Lydia herself begins on the day of her birth, September 8, 1840, in the City of Brotherly Love.

I intend to continue the search.

As I entered the final stages of the current writing, I received in my email a photograph of a beautiful portrait of Virginia Roper painted by her friend, Adele Williams. Molly had asked her older brother, who owns the painting, to photograph it for me and send it along. This was the first he had heard of the whole project, and he was excited that someone was researching "our great-grandmother, Lydia," and was especially pleased at the prospect of knowing something about "her life in Philadelphia."

Molly had to tell him, of course, that not only did we not know anything at all about the Philadelphia years, but I had struggled to dig out and assemble even a few pieces of the story of her life in Norfolk.

I emailed him, introduced myself, thanked him for the photograph, and made him a promise:

If *Looking for Lydia* is published, I will do everything I can to find Lydia Hand Bowen. I will do my best to uncover and write her story from September 8, 1840, until her departure for Norfolk, Virginia, soon after her wedding on June 7, 1865.

I will do everything I can to find her.

I will continue to tell her story.

I am not ready to give up.

This is the painting that Leighton Roper sent me; it comes with a story:

There were many weddings when Ginny Roper was a young woman; they were highly sought-after social occasions for dancing, for harmless laughter and a bit of whispering behind the potted ferns. Everyone who mattered turned out for the big weddings in Richmond.

At one of these, possibly but not certainly the wedding of Adele Williams' brother, Victor, in 1907, several of the young women were caught in a rainstorm, were soaked to the skin, and ran into the house to be stripped of their outer garments and settled in to dry before a fire.

The scene was just too much for artist Adele Williams to resist, and she took out her paints. Among her subjects was her friend, Ginny Roper, disheveled, wearing only her lace undergarments and an embroidered satin wrap, thrown hastily around her shoulders for the sake of modesty.

Unlike her social activist sister, Margaret, Lydia's youngest daughter's pursuits kept her close to home. More complex than my first impressions of her, Ginny was not only a pianist and composer who spent her time away from Norfolk mostly in the sprawling main house or in Adele Williams' studio on her family's estate at Blue Ridge Summit, Pennsylvania, she also raised Alsatians and was a trophy-winning golfer. The Roper Home Movies show Ginny swinging a golf club and feeding an ice cream cone to one of her dogs.

Unlike her mother, Ginny was a Virginia girl, born and bred in Norfolk, living out her adult life in one half of a Philadelphia "twin," or modified row house. She shared the double-house with her older sister, Margaret, until Ginny's death in 1945.

I have photographs of the double-house.

I have a photograph of John and Lydia's house on Freemason Street.

I have photographs of the house at Blue Ridge Summit.

I have a photograph of Margaret.

I have this portrait of Ginny.

I have three photographs of Lydia.

I am not ready to give up.

I am still looking for Lydia.

Acknowledgments

LOOKING FOR LYDIA; LOOKING for God has far more than a publisher. John Koehler is exactly the man Lydia Roper was looking for, and I'm pretty darned pleased with him myself. My editor at Koehler Books, Joe Coccaro, understood my objectives, corrected where necessary, made some brilliant improvements, and was willing to listen and negotiate—an unusual combination.

My gratitude to the Roper family is unlimited, but especially to Albert Roper, Molly Roper Jenkins, and Bruce Forsberg.

Stonsa Insinna's name should be plastered across the text on every page of this book. In every possible way, she saved my life. One day she drove me home; I am still here.

My first cousin, Jane Riley Gentry, has been everything but co-author. Without her close reading and courageous criticisms, it could not have been written. Terry Bowman, a friend of a little over a year, has done so much that she has asked to be identified only as my Partner in Crime. James Brookman took me on an important tour of his pinball machine collection.

Troy Valos and Bill Inge of the Sargeant Memorial Collection at Norfolk's Slover Library deserve a special thanks. They have unearthed documents and photographs, have traveled to collect them, and took care of planning and logistics for the library's celebration of Lydia and her book.

Along the way, Lydia Roper has pulled into her orbit people of such wonderful and varied qualities that all I can do is try not to forget too many. I hope anyone I do forget will make allowances for my age and general absent-mindedness. Aaron Brittain, Pastor at Talbot Park Baptist Church, in Norfolk, came up with the book's title and mentioned casting the movie as soon as he'd read one chapter; he has often kept me afloat with his irreverence, his laughter, and his startling mind. Ann Miller, administrator at the Roper Home for twenty years, shared endless stories of the Home in earlier days, and has become a good friend. Gary Barker, Rector at Kingston Episcopal Parish in Mathews, Virginia, served as emergency resource for Bible questions, bought me lunch, and donated one of his precious bromeliads. Pete Follansbee, friend, poet, and former colleague, contributed one perfect metaphor. Ellen Bunton, my first friend in the Tidewater and mother of the irrepressible "Meatball," sings the praises of the book and Isaac far and wide. Neighbors in my 1928 co-op building have offered both enthusiasm for the book and food for my frequently empty refrigerator: Lauren Leffler photographed every page of an 1894 album and made both digital and hard copies; Betsy Shelton not only read the manuscript but visited the Bible Study and makes chicken soup when I collapse; Jessica Churchill, medical student extraordinaire, posts about me on Facebook, takes care of Isaac when I'm away, and does me the great honor of trusting me.

As we neared publication, Tashawn Jones created the most wonderful website I've ever seen; I love everything about it. Debbie Holt spent a day at my house, copying and making stills from the Roper Home Movies, several of which make that website what it is. Denise Watson and The Pham created text and images for an article in the *Virginian-Pilot*. Thomas Clay Jr., aka, Slick, set up my Author Page on Facebook, and hired me to write for his blog; he introduced me to a new kind of writing and instructs me on all matters technological.

Nan Bloom and Evelyn Boyko, early members of our Bible Study, and their daughters, Diane Stabinski and Carolyn Johnson have never wavered in their loyalty. Diane and Carolyn wrote letters when they were needed.

C. Arthur Nalls III, who probably would just as soon not be

mentioned here, simply has to be mentioned here. He knows me far too well, and I am grateful.

In a temporary darkness, Anthony Radd stepped up, believed in this book, and defended it. My cousin, Edith Bates, made it possible for him to do that.

Susan Reigler, a friend of thirty years, read and actually liked the book! Wendy Marty in Michigan read, came to visit, and immediately began creating a marketing plan. And, finally, Tom Pike, my headmaster at St. Francis High School in Louisville, Kentucky, made it possible for me to put together my first class in the Bible in 1989. He changed my life in ways I'm sure he doesn't know. My lifelong study of the Bible, and so the search for Lydia, surely started there.

Book Discussion Questions

PROLOGUE AND CHAPTER ONE: *WHERE WE ARE*

1. Chapter One introduces most of the main elements of the book: the Bible; the women in the Bible Study; the Lydia Roper Home itself and a little of its history; and the mystery of Lydia Roper. Which of these do you find most interesting, and why?

2. This is a short chapter, yet four buildings are mentioned—the old building where the author lives; the Lydia Roper Home; two Methodist churches. Why so many? Do you think they are important? Why and how?

3. At the end of Chapter One, do you have a clear sense of where the book is going, of what's coming next? What keeps you reading?

CHAPTER TWO: *SETTLING IN*

1. Chapter Two's full title is "Gathering: Settling In." In what ways do the author and the women at Lydia Roper settle in?

2. Which of the women is your favorite so far? Why?

3. The chapter includes four different discussions of Scripture: Kate's question about Jesus and the Gentiles; the Prodigal Son; the angel's repeated, "Do not be afraid"; and the woman with the alabaster jar. Which discussion did you find most interesting? Which gives you the most new ways of thinking about the Bible? Which did you enjoy the most?

4. Why does the author include the business with the microphone? What does it add to the main story and ideas?

CHAPTER THREE: *HOW WE GOT HERE*

1. What do you find out about the author in this chapter: do you get to know her better? Do you like her?

2. Did you know about the two creation stories in Genesis? If so, did you learn anything new about them? If not, were you surprised?

3. There is a long section in this chapter on names and naming. How does that relate to the main idea of beginnings?

4. Discuss the unconventional ideas about Eve and the "Fall." The author says that story isn't about sin and punishment; what does she think it is about and how might that be the same as what is happening to her and to the women in the Bible Study?

5. In this chapter we get our first substantial look at the Roper family. What are your first impressions and feelings? What does the author feel about this family? How do her feelings color the narrative?

CHAPTER FOUR: *THE STORIES WE TELL*

1. Why is it so important to the author to find "stories" about Lydia Roper? Why don't the facts tell her all she needs to know?

2. Remember some of the stories told about you, or someone in your family. Are they important? Why?

3. In this chapter, the author suddenly steps in to say she's forgotten to talk about Mary Magdalene. She then tells the reader her plans for changing the schedule. Is this

bit of "schoolteacher" talk a distraction? Does it serve a purpose?

4. Kate pops up with one of her questions—a hard one. What does it mean to be saved? Whose answer do you prefer, the Baptist preacher's or the Episcopal priest's? Why?

5. Do you agree with the author, or with the author's friend, about asking "disturbing" personal questions of women in their nineties?

6. What do you think about the process of scriptural reading called *lectio divina*? Have you ever tried it? Would you like to?

7. Why do you think the author writes so much about Cora Mae?

8. Describe the 1894 album edited by Margaret Roper. Why is it so exciting to the author?

CHAPTERS FIVE THROUGH EIGHT: *THE LADIES*

1. The next four chapters are much shorter and more focused than Chapters One through Four. Do you find this sudden shift confusing or an interesting break from the previous longer chapters?

2. The women who are included here are Catherine, Nan, Terry, Kate, Inez, Evelyn, Lucille, Neal, and Cora Mae. Now that you're learning a little more about them, which of the women do you like the best? About which do you have the most questions?

3. In these chapters, the author places the three photographs she has found of Lydia so far: a picture of a very young girl, no more than fifteen; a photograph of Lydia at around eighty (both hang in Molly's house in Lynchburg); and a family portrait of Lydia, John, their son, William, and his baby daughter, Elizabeth,

taken in 1900. Lydia would have been sixty, John sixty-five. This last came from Bruce Forsberg, one of Lydia and John's great-granddaughters; the baby is Bruce's mother, Elizabeth. Why does she choose to put those photographs into these chapters? Do they give you a feeling of knowing Lydia a bit better, or not?

4. What are some possible ways of understanding the line, "So many of the women here need calling back"?

CHAPTER NINE: *THE HOUSES WE BUILD*

1. What would you say all these places have in common: The Lydia Roper Home; houses Captain Roper built for his family; the house the author's parents built; the Ark of the Covenant; the Tabernacle; the Jerusalem Temple; the Garden of Eden and the Promised Land; Robert Frost's "Wall;" an Anchor Hold; the Children's Hospital of the King's Daughters; and the inn where Joseph and Mary found no room?

2. What do you think the author means when she writes, "I know that our relationship to those places we inhabit and leave and for which we search is the informing metaphor of the spiritual life in any tradition and is, in fact, the governing reality in our lives."

3. What purpose is served by including a paragraph like the following:

> I spent eight months of 2013 as a resident of the Lydia Roper Home. I know every room, every hallway, every plumbing problem, every furnace crisis; I stood in the community bathroom on the second floor and covered my ears against the shrieking of the alarm during fire drills. I sat in the hallway outside the dining room, waiting for someone to sound the chime. I waited to be handed my medications by the technician on duty. I put my laundry outside my door?

CHAPTER TEN: *JUST ANOTHER WEDNESDAY*

1. This chapter opens with an echo of the first paragraph in the book. Did you recognize the wording right away? There are obvious differences between the two paragraphs: what are they and what impact do they have on your understanding of the book as this final chapter begins?

2. Is the photograph of the author's cat, Isaac, effective? Why or why not?

3. What are some of the changes the author describes both in the Bible Study and in other areas?

4. In the Scriptures, this chapter focuses on The Acts of the Apostles and Paul's Letter to the Galatians, and on the two luminaries, Peter and Paul. What changes have occurred in the biblical story since the end of the three Synoptic Gospels?

5. Does the author like Paul? How can you tell? Do the ladies in the Bible Study like Paul?

EPILOGUE

List three or four things that the Epilogue adds to the book's end.

THOUGHTS AFTER THE LAST CURTAIN: *WHERE WE GO FROM HERE*

The book's final section proposes a sequel to *Looking for Lydia; Looking for God*. What, specifically, might this sequel have to offer and is it something you might be interested in reading?